SØREN KIERKEGAARD
AND THE COMMON MAN

SØREN KIERKEGAARD AND THE COMMON MAN

Jørgen Bukdahl

Translated, revised, edited,
and with notes by

Bruce H. Kirmmse

William B. Eerdmans Publishing Company
Grand Rapids, Michigan / Cambridge, U.K.

Originally published as
Søren Kierkegaard og den menige mand
© 1961 Munksgaard Forlag, Copenhagen

This edition © 2001 Wm. B. Eerdmans Publishing Co.
All rights reserved

Wm. B. Eerdmans Publishing Co.
255 Jefferson Ave. S.E., Grand Rapids, Michigan 49503 /
P.O. Box 163, Cambridge CB3 9PU U.K.

Printed in the United States of America

06 05 04 03 02 01   7 6 5 4 3 2 1

Library of Congress Cataloging-in-Publication Data

Bukdahl, Jørgen, 1896-1982.
[Søren Kierkegaard og den menige mand. English]
Søren Kierkegaard and the common man / Jørgen Bukdahl;
translated, revised, edited, and with notes by Bruce H. Kirmmse.
p.   cm.
ISBN 0-8028-4738-2 (alk. paper)
1. Kierkegaard, Søren, 1813-1855.
I. Kirmmse, Bruce H.   II. Title.

BR4377.B813   2001
198′.9 — dc21

2001023813

www.eerdmans.com

Contents

Translator's Preface and Acknowledgments

The author of this book, Jørgen Bukdahl (1896-1982), was a popular educator and lecturer as well as an author of many books on subjects ranging from philosophy and religion to art and politics. Bukdahl was rooted in the broadly democratic Danish tradition of popular enlightenment that grew out of the "folk high school" movement of the nineteenth century, which in turn can trace its origins to the religious and educational vision of N. F. S. Grundtvig (1783-1872).

The subject of Bukdahl's study, Søren Kierkegaard (1813-55), witnessed the triumph of modern mass society in his native Denmark and in Europe generally, and he was a perceptive and trenchant critic of its shortcomings, particularly when an existing social and political order attempted to legitimize itself by cloaking itself in religion. But Kierkegaard did not take sides in politics as such. After Kierkegaard's death his intellectual heirs fought over the meaning of his legacy. Atheists and freethinking "modernists" tried to claim him as their own and assimilate him to the "Left," while anti-modernist conservatives tried to enlist him in the battle of the "Right" against popular sovereignty. By the time the Cold War reached its height in the decades after World War II, things seemed to have settled down, and after a final attempt by the atheistic existentialists of the "Left" to claim Kierkegaard for themselves, the "Right" appeared to have counterattacked successfully, due in no small measure to the undeniably religious character of Kierkegaard's works. The only problem was that the actual historical Kierkegaard had been lost in the battle.

vii

The purpose of Bukdahl's series of lectures on Kierkegaard, which later became the present book, *Søren Kierkegaard and the Common Man* (first published in Danish in 1961 as *Søren Kierkegaard og den menige mand*), was to rescue Kierkegaard from the arch-conservative caricature to which the factional warfare had relegated him. Kierkegaard, after all, was both a brilliant thinker and an actual human being, and the nuances of his position were too complicated to be forced into any simple category. He was an historical person embedded in a particular society at a particular time and cannot be properly understood dislodged from his context. Bukdahl's book placed Kierkegaard splendidly in his times and provided a welcome respite from the ahistorical caricatures that had dominated the scene.

I discovered this book a number of years ago, when I was doing the research that resulted in my book *Kierkegaard in Golden Age Denmark* (Indiana University Press, 1990). In that work I was happy to acknowledge my indebtedness to Jørgen Bukdahl. Bukdahl's daughter, Else Marie Bukdahl, subsequently read my book and noted my appreciation of her father's work. When she asked me to undertake the project of translating this book, I agreed to do so both because it constitutes a milestone in our contemporary understanding of Kierkegaard and because it is a delightful book in its own right. I am happy to be able to help gain for this book the broader readership that it deserves.

The present English translation differs in several minor respects from the Danish original. Changes in wording have been necessitated by Jørgen Bukdahl's popular and discursive style, but this English version is faithful to the meaning of the Danish original. Similarly, an occasional flourish or digression has been omitted. Bukdahl often cited Kierkegaard rather loosely and occasionally omitted important portions of a cited passage's context. In every case, cited passages from Kierkegaard have been verified and where necessary emended. As a Dane, Bukdahl was able to make offhand references to Danish historical events and cultural figures whose significance may not be clear to the non-Danish reader. I have added a biographical introduction to provide some details of Kierkegaard's historical context. In addition, where it has seemed necessary or helpful, explanatory wording has been worked into the text or supplemental notes have been added to help clarify things taken for granted in Denmark but not generally known by non-Danes. Where they had no connection with the argument developed in the book, several casual references to Danish cultural figures or events have simply been omitted. Full documentation has also been supplied for Bukdahl's citations from authors other than Kierkegaard, and in every instance the citation has been checked against the original source. All references have been consigned to the endnotes, and every effort has been made to keep this book as informal and accessible as the original Danish version. Unless otherwise specified, all endnotes are by the translator and editor. A brief guide to Kierkegaard's writings in English translation has been substituted for Bukdahl's bibliographical postscript, and his epilogue has been omitted.

I am very thankful to Diane Teddye Birmingham for valuable assistance in proofreading, to Morten Brøgger and Iben Thranholm Madsen for helping to verify references to Kierkegaard's works and papers, to Flemming Lundgreen-Nielsen for helping to track down Grundtvig references, and to Margaret Ryan Hellman, whose careful editorial eye has been over the entire text. I am happy to thank the Danish National Research Council for the Humanities [Statens humanistiske forskningsråd], the University of Copenhagen, the Søren Kierkegaard Research Centre, and the R. Francis Johnson Fund of Connecticut College for the support that made it possible to complete this translation.

Bruce H. Kirmmse

Biographical Introduction
to the English Language Edition

O ver the course of Søren Kierkegaard's lifetime (1813-55), his native Denmark was transformed from an early modern society (a rather rigid, hierarchical, but "face-to-face" absolute monarchy) into a modern mass society based on the anonymous forces of the marketplace and popular sovereignty. Kierkegaard's Denmark thus witnessed the ascendancy of "the common man"[1] over a society that had been governed by visible elites. Thus Denmark in Kierkegaard's time gave him occasion to consider carefully the crucial role ordinary people would play in this new era, and this is the focus of the present book.

Søren Aabye Kierkegaard was the seventh and last child of Michael Pedersen Kierkegaard (1756-1838) and Ane Sørensdatter Lund Kierkegaard (1768-1834), both of whom came from impoverished peasant families in Jutland. At the age of fourteen, M. P. Kierkegaard had gone off to Copenhagen to seek his fortune, and he indeed found it, becoming a well-to-do dry goods merchant, able to live off his investments by the time he was forty. The Kierkegaard children were raised in the comfortable surroundings of the solid bourgeoisie, and two of the sons, Peter Christian and Søren Aabye, were given a first-rate education at one of Copenhagen's finest preparatory schools and at the University of Copenhagen.

Yet the Kierkegaard family home was marked not only by upward mobility but also by a stubborn sense of its peasant origins and a continuing loyalty to the rural religiosity that had seized much of the eighteenth- and nineteenth-century peasantry, often in explicit (and political) defiance of the dry official religion of the urban cultural elite. In the Kierkegaard household, as in many other middle-class Copenhagen households only a generation or two removed from the soil, this dissent-tinged Christianity found institutional expression by membership in the city's thriving *Herrnhut* [Moravian Brethren] congregation. But the Kierkegaard family hedged its bet and participated enthusiastically not only in the devotional meetings of the Moravians but also in the elegant services of the official state church, presided over by the urbane Pastor (later Bishop) J. P. Mynster (1775-1854). The split between country and city, between peasant and elite culture, was summed up neatly in the tension between the Moravian congregation and state church.

After his preparatory education, Kierkegaard matriculated into the University of Copenhagen in 1831, and in accordance with his father's wishes he followed the path of his elder brother Peter Christian by pursuing a degree in theology. Typically such a degree was a stepping-stone to a career in the state church (which constituted the largest market for university graduates), a path that appeared to hold out the promise of both divine approval and a secure, comfortable livelihood. Kierkegaard's father was not alone in perceiving the advantages of studying theology: in Kierkegaard's time the Theology Faculty enrolled by far the greatest number of university students, accounting for approximately half of the roughly one thousand students at the university. But the Theology Faculty did not provide Kierkegaard with the intellectual and spiritual sustenance he craved, and he found greater support on the Philosophy Faculty, particularly from F. C. Sibbern (1785-1872), a multifaceted professor of philosophy, and Poul Martin Møller (1794-1838), an author and professor of philosophy, who was by all accounts an extraordinarily sympathetic personality. Not surprisingly, when Kierkegaard decided to take an advanced degree, it was not in theology but in philosophy, with a dissertation entitled *On the Concept of Irony*.

There was in fact a multiplicity of factors that contributed to Kierkegaard's decision to abandon his original plan of a career in the church. One such factor was the dry, academic character of the Theology Faculty already mentioned. Of even greater importance were the conflicts that wracked the church itself. Bishop J. P. Mynster, whose quasi-Romantic, personal Christianity had been a breath of fresh air in the rationalistic Enlightenment atmosphere that had dominated the state church at the beginning of the century, now ruled over the church with an iron hand. The rise of peasant literacy and a mass democratic movement in officially absolutist Denmark put the Danish state church on the defensive during the whole of Kierkegaard's period. Bishop Mynster — along with his successor, Bishop H. L. Martensen, who had earlier been Kierkegaard's tutor at the university — felt compelled to use the full legal apparatus of the state in order to combat the various popular religious movements that sprang up, movements that the conservative representatives of the old regime rightly recognized as not only religious but also political. These movements began with the rise of uneducated lay preachers among the peasantry, but they spread to the capital with the fiery preaching of the learned Jacob Christian Lindberg (1797-1857). Ultimately, however, the largest portion of the religious revolt against the status quo in the established church found its focus in N. F. S. Grundtvig (1783-1872), the volcanic and prolific personality who became the spokesman for a constantly evolving vision of a new synthesis between a revived Christianity and a democratic culture. Søren Kierkegaard's family was interested in Lindberg but kept its distance. Søren's cautiously idealistic older brother Peter Christian eventually emerged as a moderate partisan of Grundtvig's movement. Søren, on the other hand, could never get past the bombastic, theatrical side of Grundtvig, which he viewed as self-indulgence or worse. In the end, the Grundtvigians remained within the state church — which after the democratic revolution of 1848 had been renamed (ominously, in Søren's view) the "People's Church" — as a sort of left-populist wing, and Peter Christian became a bishop. Søren Kierkegaard could choose neither ecclesiastical alternative, neither the conservative wing of Mynster and Martensen nor the democratic wing of Grundtvig and his own brother. Kierkegaard's Christianity was destined to be the disestablished, "unofficial" Christianity of an outsider. In Kierkegaard's view, the Christianity of the ordinary person (the "common man") of this new, democratic age had to be that of an individual, not that of a religious movement or party that would of necessity be compelled to make compromises.

There were other forces pulling Kierkegaard away from a career in the state church. The new Romantic philosophy of the individual genius, of the innermost soul as the seat of selfhood, had come to Denmark early in the nineteenth century in the person of Henrich Steffens (1773-1845), who served as the precursor of the remarkable outpouring of literature and philosophy known as the "Golden Age." This Romantic Danish renaissance was varied in the extreme, from the religious poetry and ecstatic essays of Grundtvig to the scientific experiments and *Naturphilosophie* of Hans Christian Ørsted (1777-1850), the magical lyricism of the poet Adam Oehlenschlæger (1779-1850), the brilliant pseudo-naiveté of the fairy tales and novels of Hans Christian Andersen (1805-75), and the witty plays, poetry, and aesthetic essays of Johan Ludvig Heiberg (1791-1860), who together with his novelist mother, Thomasine Gyllembourg (1773-1856), and his wife, the actress Johanne Luise Heiberg (1812-90), constituted the leading family and the epicenter of high culture during the period. For Kierkegaard, who had a tortured on-again, off-again relationship with these "coteries of culture," as he called them, one lesson of the Golden Age was irrefutable: the path to reality was an inward path, which led to and through the self. Furthermore, for Kierkegaard, as for the Golden Age generally, this path to authenticity was a *literary* path. But just as Kierkegaard could not become an ordinary theologian, so was he incapable of becoming just another Golden Age literary figure. In this new democratic age of "the common man," Kierkegaard insisted that the task set for himself and for every person unconditionally was to become one's own, singular self, full and unabridged. For Kierkegaard this ultimately meant becoming neither a respectable pastor nor a member of the reigning literary coterie, but a "religious writer."

Learning his vocation was painful for Kierkegaard. After the completion of his theological degree, in keeping with the expectations normal for men of his age and station, Kierkegaard became engaged to be married to a lovely young woman of his own social class. Indeed, Regine Olsen (1822-1904) was not merely of Kierkegaard's social class (or even a bit above it); her family also belonged to the same Moravian congregation to which Kierkegaard's family and many of his friends belonged, and she thus shared some of the religious and cultural tensions and ambiguities that marked her fiancé's background. But soon Kierkegaard came to feel that the path on which he had already embarked was too tortuous, too solitary, too uniquely his own to share intimately with anyone else, and after thirteen months he broke off the engagement, an action that produced scandal, shame, and embarrassment for all parties concerned.

By the end of September 1841, Kierkegaard was free again, his engagement broken, his dissertation *On the Concept of Irony* successfully defended, and he was on his way to Berlin, from which he returned less than a year later with the bulk of the manuscript of his great breakthrough work, *Either/Or*. Kierkegaard's dazzlingly productive career as a writer had begun. Between February 1843, when *Either/Or* appeared, and the appearance of *Practice in Christianity* in September 1850, most of Kierkegaard's enormous corpus was published, including virtually all the most famous of his writings (such as *Fear and Trembling, Repetition, Stages on Life's Way, The Concept of Anxiety, Philosophical Fragments, Concluding Unscientific Postscript, Works of Love, Christian Discourses,* and *The Sickness Unto Death*) plus a host of less well-known pseudonymous and edifying writings. Remarkably, he also produced an equal or greater volume of unpublished papers and journals.

Kierkegaard's career as a writer was not without its difficulties. He believed that much of his work was not accorded the serious attention he felt it merited, a grievance that is by and large justified when one examines the quantity and quality of the critical attention with which the Danish Golden Age greeted Kierkegaard's works. On the other hand, there was much about Kierkegaard's work that was unprecedented, both in its form and its contents. His work was virtually impossible to classify. Was it literature? Philosophy? Religious apologetics? Who was qualified to review it? When Kierkegaard did manage to get into the spotlight it was in a most unpleasant fashion, in 1846, when his work, and even more his person, was made the butt of merciless lampoon and satire in a popular periodical called *The Corsair*. It is true that Kierkegaard had to some extent provoked this attack by breaching the code of journalistic etiquette in unmasking a pseudonymous author of whom he disapproved, and it is true, furthermore, that Kierkegaard had baited *The Corsair* and publicly begged it to come after him. Still, the meanness and the tenacity of the public punishment meted out by the journal was disproportionate to the insult Kierkegaard had inflicted, and this provided him with many opportunities to bemoan his fate (privately, in his journals), comparing his suffering to that endured by martyrs and other innocent victims. *The Corsair* was edited by Meïr Aron Goldschmidt (1819-87), a maverick writer who was nearly as unclassifiable as Kierkegaard himself. Goldschmidt, a Jew and thus an outsider in polite Golden Age Denmark, started as a brilliant, cheeky author and a radical critic, and it was in this incarnation that he edited the journal in which Kierkegaard was roasted. In his later career Goldschmidt emerged as a thoughtful conservative, and he came to lament the cruelty with which Kierkegaard had been pursued.

During the 1850s Kierkegaard published much less, though his writing continued unabated. As it turned out, he was storing up material to be unleashed in a scathing critique of the established church and of "Christendom" — that is, what Kierkegaard regarded as the unholy marriage of Christianity and the existing social order — that appeared during the last year of his life. Perhaps the real change had come in 1848, when Denmark underwent a revolution — the only European revolution of that year not to be subsequently reversed. Suddenly the nation was transformed from an absolute monarchy, in which the king's word was the sole source of law, into a popular sovereignty state, in which law could only be made by a democratically elected legislature chosen on the basis of what was at that time probably the broadest franchise in the world. This was an earthquake. The age of the "common man" had indeed arrived.

But it was clear to Kierkegaard, as to many others, that this was not merely an earthquake in the political sense: in the near future, all cultural configurations would be "democratized." Economic relations, transportation, communication, literature, the arts, the media, education, and, yes, religion would be transformed. Kierkegaard wrote that 1848 marked the greatest transformation since the end of classical antiquity. The age of the "common man" meant that the individual person's very sense of selfhood was on the table for discussion. What, or whom, would we become? As has been noted, Kierkegaard thought the renaming of the state church as the People's Church a particularly troubling development. In the old days, the common people were under no illusions that the state church was *their* church. It was the church of the king and the aristocrats, of the capital and its snobbish cultural elite, and of the pastors (all of whom were trained in

Copenhagen) who often controlled the largest farms in the district. Not infrequently the common people lived in an adversarial relation to the official church. They had their own Christianity: their own preachers, often arrested; their own prayer books and hymnals, often banned; their own religious assemblies, often broken up by the police. They could protest against the religious tyranny of the state church in the name of true Christianity and of "the people." But now that Denmark had become a democratic country, now that the people legally owned the state and the government, now that the church had become the *People's* Church (though with no change in personnel and little in policy) — in whose name *now* could the people protest the religious tyranny (and for Kierkegaard, the spiritless mediocrity) of the established church?

This was what prompted Kierkegaard to break his silence at the end of 1854 and to burst upon the scene as the articulate and incandescent enemy of the dangerously self-congratulatory nonsense he labeled "Christendom." The proximate cause was the succession of H. L. Martensen to the post of Bishop of Zealand and Primate of the Danish People's Church. After serving as Kierkegaard's tutor, Martensen had moved on to become a popular and successful professor of theology who mediated between the Hegelianism of his friend and cultural ally Heiberg on the one hand, and the worried "orthodoxy" of Bishop Mynster and various mainstream theologians on the other. Martensen had proven an adept church politician and, following Mynster's death earlier in the year, had managed to get his nomination as head of the People's Church forced through — over the objections of the king himself — by his political allies, who were then in charge of a short-lived conservative coalition government. The established church — the *People's* Church, of all things — would henceforth be governed by such political conniving.

This was too much for Kierkegaard. Quite apart from his personal dissatisfaction with Martensen, Mynster, and others, the prospect that Christianity might now become synonymous with "the Danish People's Church" — that democracy might bestow upon "official Christianity" a legitimacy that absolutism had been unable to attain — seemed to Kierkegaard an unprecedented danger. What Kierkegaard called "the Christianity of the New Testament" could *never* be synonymous with any worldly set of compromises and institutions. The new age of "the common man," which Kierkegaard acknowledged and even welcomed in its various political, social, and material manifestations — and of which Kierkegaard was himself a part — must not come to mean *"vox populi vox dei."* This was Kierkegaard's final and most emphatic point, and he died insisting upon it.

CHAPTER ONE

Internal Self-Definition

Romanticism is a rather unwieldy term. It denotes both a complex set of ideas and also that period when seeds germinated that had been planted during the Enlightenment, seeds of reaction against the Enlightenment attitude toward Reason, emphasizing the primacy of feeling and fantasy.

But the central tendency of the Romantic movement, which flooded the arid earth of the Enlightenment like the life-giving waters of the Nile, was its call for "internal self-definition." Internal self-definition means understanding oneself as an individual before relating to the many and to society. It means the excitement of feeling oneself supported by a rich inner world, a world saturated with fantasy and emotion, though also saturated with Reason, which is something more than mere understanding. The Romantic movement fostered the cult of genius and also the cult of the innocent and cheerful child of Nature. Nature and Spirit, the old antagonists, once again teased philosophers into trying to capture reality and explain life with great objective systems. We see systems of this sort throughout the nineteenth century in the works of Schelling, Hegel, Comte, and Marx. But if the call for internal self-definition produced great philosophical systems, it also developed into a subjectivism and individualism that provided the raw materials for a philosophy of personality. In Denmark this personalistic philosophy found expression in such thinkers as Poul Martin Møller[1] and F. C. Sibbern,[2] each of whom started from fundamentally Christian concepts and each of whom, though committed

1

to personalism, tried in different ways to oppose the anarchy that results from subjectivism and individualism.

Whether understood as a systematic philosophy or as a philosophy of personality, the internal definition of the self is connected to the development or unfolding of the inner world, which is in turn accompanied by both a growing self-consciousness and changes in the external conditions of the human race. This is the idea of progress that formed the basis of the humanism — that confidence in the manifold possibilities of human development and organization — that undergirded the nineteenth century all the way up to World War I. The notion of internal self-definition also found support in the new sense of history that had been awakened by Johann von Herder. Special emphasis was given to the living sources of history within a people — myth, legend, fairy tales, and folk songs — that the speculative philosophers viewed as the source of both religion and science.

While the contents of this Romanticism overflow their vessel, and many weighty volumes have been written about Romanticism without clearly identifying its basic concepts and categories, it would be safe to characterize Romanticism as the human spirit's mightiest attempt at self-redemption since the Renaissance. And it was also the greatest attempt, in religious disguise, to contest the anthropology of the Gospels, in particular by allegorizing that anthropology and establishing a sort of reconciliation between humanism and Christianity. The first poetic expression of this was Adam Oehlenschlæger's[3] "The Life of Jesus Christ Repeated in the Annual Cycle of Nature" (1805). A philosophical expression of this attempt at reconciliation can be found in Hans Christian Ørsted's[4] *The Spirit in Nature* (1850). Then came the speculative attempt of H. L. Martensen,[5] and finally liberal theology.

This Romanticism, with its insistence on internal self-definition and its attacks from two different directions — employing subjectivism and individualism on the one hand, and an objective system on the other — constituted both the positive and (especially) the negative impetus for the work of Søren Kierkegaard. During the heady years of his youth, which Kierkegaard wrote about in the first three volumes of his journals, it was with the help of Socrates in particular that he was liberated from the dialectic of Romanticism. The term "dialectic" stems from Hegel and from

2

late Romanticism, when the pathos of high Romanticism, rooted in the tension between Spirit and Nature, came to be replaced by the reflective, the interesting, the piquant — in short, by the dialectical play of which Kierkegaard more than anyone was master.

Like N. F. S. Grundtvig[6] before him (in his *World History,* published in 1812), Kierkegaard realized that he was engaged in a war on two fronts, against both of Romanticism's tendencies, the subjective and the objective. "The subjectively existing thinker is therefore just as bifrontal as is the situation of existence itself," he wrote in the *Concluding Unscientific Postscript.*[7] For those who have insisted that Kierkegaard's requirement of subjectivity was connected with the subjectivism and individualism of the nineteenth century, the duality in his position has proven difficult to discern. But Kierkegaard himself denigrated the subjectivism of his times as subjectivism in the wrong sense.

His battle on these two fronts was inseparable from his most fundamental intention, to seek out *reality.* Kierkegaard's charge against the philosophy and the Christianity of his times was that they lacked a sense of reality, which in turn was rooted in a lack of honesty. He believed people fled the requirements of reality, taking refuge in a life of habit, of rote Christianity, in which the only remaining trace of obligation to the authority of the Gospels was a bit of suggestive terminology. He saw them take refuge in a bourgeois philistinism devoid of pathos, slack and indolent, intoxicated with aesthetic enjoyment or speculative fantasy.

The whole of Kierkegaard's writings can be seen as one sustained attempt to isolate and define reality as the internal self-definition of the personality. If this self-definition is successfully carried out, he believed, a person is "real," and is in charge of the inner life of the soul as well as of his or her domestic, civic, and private affairs. In ethical terms, internal self-definition of the personality comes when an individual goes beyond what has been thought in order to *exist* in that thought. Seen from this point of view, it is an illumination and interpretation of the mystery of free will. In religious terms, the internal self-definition of the personality can also be defined as the point at which a person encounters the concrete demands of God. Seen from this point of view, it is an interpretation of the peculiar powerlessness and vulnerability of an individual in the world.[8]

In espousing the notion that reality is the personality's grasp of itself, Kierkegaard was a child of both Romanticism and the eighteenth century. From the Romantics he gained a sense for the inner world of the personality. From the eighteenth century he learned that decisive significance could not be attributed to what he called life's "differences" — one's particular intellectual talents and capacities — but to one's responsible relationship to those particulars. The antitheses of the world stood firm; Kierkegaard, like Grundtvig, stood unwaveringly on the principle of contradiction.[9] Antitheses — good and evil, right and wrong — cannot be volatilized by speculative synthesis; they must be respected in the either/or of choice. In insisting on this, Kierkegaard exploded the evolutionary thinking of Romanticism. A human being exists in choice and thus develops by leaps that speculation cannot discern.

In Kierkegaard's writings, human freedom is not simply Romanticism's infinitization of a personality in the self-development of thought and fantasy. It is a person's relation to himself or herself as pure possibility, as a task for ethical choice. But at the same time, freedom is not to be used to lift oneself above the petty accidents of one's surroundings, to take the leap of genius out of everyday life. The meaning of freedom is precisely to accept one's concreteness, and to transform it from a constricting necessity into a capacious reality. Freedom thus means taking a responsible posture with respect to the entirety of one's given life, for only in that way will the entire aesthetic content of life be preserved. And however different the gifts and talents of different individuals may be, all are equal in their freedom to manage and develop their gifts.

By radicalizing the idea of freedom in this way, and by emphasizing the ethical task with which each person is confronted, Kierkegaard was able to insist upon an unabridged religious notion of equality. This sense of freedom and equality was well known in the eighteenth century, and here Kierkegaard had his roots in Kant. Kierkegaard's approach to freedom and equality was the antithesis of Romanticism, which made freedom into an ability, a talent, a need that could be developed, and replaced equality with an emphasis on special privileges for the talented, for the coteries of the cultivated elite. Instead of equality, the Romantic notion of freedom displayed a disdain for the common people, and with the condescension of a superior it permitted them to partake of the few crumbs that fell from the table of cultivation.

In sum, the general inclination of Kierkegaard's argument was that a person can only earn aesthetic validity by obeying the ethical requirements of existence. As a goal in and of itself, the aesthetic only subverts itself. Equilibrium between the aesthetic and the ethical in the composition of the personality can only be achieved by attaining the ethical. This notion of equilibrium was Kierkegaard's unique combination of eighteenth-century ethical and nineteenth-century aesthetic views.

So much for viewing Kierkegaard's position and his intent through the prism of internal self-definition (the fundamental category of Romanticism) and with reference to the notions of equality which were rooted in the eighteenth century. We will now see how all of this is related to one of the principal problems in Kierkegaard's writings, namely, the question of the simple person, or what he called "the common man."

CHAPTER TWO

Henrich Steffens: The Way to Myth and Fairy Tale

"The internal definition of the self and the theatre of conflict from which it emerges victorious" was the subject of the legendary lecture that Henrich Steffens[1] gave at Eler's Hall at the University of Copenhagen in 1802. At the time of the lecture Søren Kierkegaard had not yet been born, of course, but when he read it subsequently he was better able to understand the philosophical problem with which the lecture dealt and the conclusion it reached than was the generation of the original audience, carried away as it had been by the lecture's evocative tone. Kierkegaard owned most of Steffens's scholarly works and was always captivated by them, as he was by Steffens's short stories and his ten volumes of memoirs, *What I Experienced* (1841-44), which he also owned.

In the first of his 1802 lectures, Steffens spoke of an obscure instinct toward unity which saturates the whole of existence:

> If we observe this instinct of unity we notice: 1) that it must be infinite, like the universe itself; 2) that, viewed from our present standpoint, it must be *differentiated* from the egoistic instinct, as it is indeed the *antithesis* of that instinct; and 3) that therefore, seen from one point of view, it tends to abolish all *individuality as such.*
>
> But this instinct itself only exists to the extent that the individual exists, and it is nothing other than the expression of the unity of all individuality. Thus, in seeking to maintain itself it contradicts and

7

abolishes itself. If everything is dissolved into individuals, then the individual itself cannot exist, because the individual exists only in connection with the *whole*. If everything is dissolved into infinite unity — a unity opposed to the individual — then that unity itself cannot exist, because it is nothing but the unity of all individualities.

Indeed, life is infested, so to speak, with contradictions of this sort. How can the single individual exist in the face of an infinite and all-powerful instinct toward unity that seems to engulf it? How can the whole exist in the face of a deeply ingrained egoistic instinct that arms every individual against the whole and all individuals against one another? How can two principles that conflict with and annul one another — the first principle, which gives us multiplicity, individuals, and the finite; and the second principle, which gives us *the one,* the universal, and the infinite — how can they unite, penetrate one another, and from this complete fusion produce the same Being, Existence, *Life?* This is completely inconceivable to us and is surely the highest problem of philosophy.[2]

That this was in fact a philosophy of existence cloaked in the rhetoric and speculation of Romanticism was clear to Kierkegaard. In this he differed from the first generation of Romantics, who had been swept up in the current of rhetoric and carried off by an enthusiastic feeling of redemption. Kierkegaard took particular note of Steffens's remarks near the end of his lecture:

Our first view of all this shows us that everything exists in an eternal and unceasing struggle between opposite tendencies. And how are we ourselves situated? Of necessity, we are involved in that struggle, a struggle demanding our every effort. We must fight for ourselves, as is demanded by the egoistic instinct. We must fight for the whole, as is commanded by morality. Everyone knows his or her duties. Human beings are made for action, not for speculation. Time and the onward movement of culture have entangled the human race in contradictions that only action can give us any hope of resolving, if not entirely, then at least in part.[3]

These remarks provided Kierkegaard with the materials he would need in his musings about Romanticism, Romantic dialectic, and concealed irony, all of which were important in his early unpublished writings. Steffens also laid the groundwork for the polemical position Kierkegaard adopted in his dissertation *On the Concept of Irony,* especially in his great chapter on Plato and myth, which was inspired by Steffens.[4] Steffens himself dealt with myth in his seventh lecture, which gave N. F. S. Grundtvig the impetus for his own research into myths. The lecture described the age of myth as a time when word and action were one, a notion that Steffens later incorporated into the introduction to his *Caricatures of What Is Most Holy* (1819-21). This latter work of Steffens was the one that most captivated Kierkegaard, who borrowed it, read it, and immediately thereafter purchased his own copy.

Steffens's influence on Kierkegaard is clear from the earliest volumes of Kierkegaard's papers.[5] Thus he could write, "What I call the mythological-poetical element in history is the aura that hovers over every genuine historical endeavor; it is not an abstraction, not prosaic actuality, but a *transfiguration,* and every genuine historical trend will also give birth to such a mythological idea."[6] His journals also contain his reflections on mythology as the idea of eternity captured within the categories of time and space. During the most decisive years of his youth (1835-36) this led Kierkegaard to the study of semi-mythical, ideal figures: Faust, in particular, as well as Ahasuerus (the "Wandering Jew") and Don Juan. Kierkegaard's interest in mythology during his formative years is reflected in his journal notes on aesthetics, which take up nearly one hundred printed pages.[7] For the most part these notes deal with Faust — not only with Goethe's figure, but also with the relation between Goethe's symbolic-realistic version of Faust (as the personification of doubt) and the Faust character as depicted in folk tales, thus maintaining the dialectic between the wise and the simple. Kierkegaard asked if Goethe's version is a drama of immediacy, as Johan Ludvig Heiberg claimed. He concluded that Goethe is not *in* it; he has lived through it and is now lifted above it. Goethe's irony and humor is "as though lightning and thunder were being viewed by someone who is elevated above it on a mountaintop. . . . *It is strange to see the younger generation, which certainly has something Faustian about itself, fasten onto Goethe's version of the story,* which is anything but seductive . . . it is rather as if Goethe were the gray man in Peter Schlemihl, who took out of his pocket the shadow of Faust, which said: 'justo judicio Dei damnatus sum'."[8] Kierkegaard remembered this six years later when he wrote *Either/ Or,* in which he explained Don Juan as the expression of the demonic as the sensuous element and Faust as the expression of the demonic as the spiritual element excluded by the spirit of Christianity. In connection with a popular little book about Faust on sale at a local shop, Kierkegaard wrote that at a time when people were so preoccupied with Faust, when each university tutor or professor made a practice of publishing books about Faust and of repeating

> what has already been said by all the other graduates and scholarly confirmands, then he thinks he may ignore an insignificant, ordinary little book like this. It never occurs to him how beautiful it is that, after all, the truly great things are the common property of everyone, that a peasant lad goes to [the bookseller] Tribler's widow or a ballad monger at the Haymarket and reads [this little book] to himself under his breath at the same time that Goethe is writing his *Faust.* And indeed, this ordinary book is worthy of notice. Above all, it has what people praise as a noble quality in a wine: it has bouquet, . . . and when one opens it, one encounters such a spicy, delicious, and unique fragrance that one gets quite an extraordinary feeling.[9]

During these decisive years of Kierkegaard's ferment (1835-36), Steffens's book served as both a direct and an indirect inspiration. He was influenced not only by Steffens's philosophy, with its campaign against speculation and its tendency toward the existential, but also by Steffens's reflections on the specific contributions of Johann von Herder: mythology, myth, and folk song as expressions of an age of simplicity, a time when religion and poetry, word and deed, were bound together. Kierkegaard would no more forget this Romantic influence than would Grundtvig, whose two volumes of mythology Kierkegaard owned, along with his *Danish Proverbs and Sayings.* Kierkegaard's collection of fairy tales, legends, and folk songs was as large as his collection of Danish literature.

In this same period, Kierkegaard wrote two of his longest and most candid letters, mapping out his thoughts on a variety of subjects. One was written to a relative, the naturalist Peter Wilhelm Lund,[10] and another was to a friend, Peter Engel Lind.[11] In the letter to Lund, Kierkegaard expressed his enthusiasm for the natural sciences, "but I would not make them my principal field of study. By virtue of reason and freedom, life has always interested me most. It has been my abiding wish to clarify and solve the riddle of life." This was accompanied by a long reflection on Faust:

> For many people, this Faustian element asserts itself to a greater or lesser degree in every intellectual development, which is why it has always seemed to me that the world-historical significance of Faust ought to be acknowledged. Just as our ancestors had a goddess of longing, I believe that Faust represents the personification of doubt. He need not be more than that, and it is probably a violation of the [Faustian] idea when Goethe has him undergo conversion. . . . For although Mephistopheles has indeed permitted him to peer through his spectacles and to look into human beings and into the hidden depths of the earth, Faust is always compelled to entertain doubts about Mephistopheles, because the latter could not enlighten him about the most profound intellectual matters. In accordance with his idea, Faust could never turn to God, for at the very moment that he did so he would have to admit to himself that this was where he could truly find enlightenment. But at that very instant, he would of course have denied his character as a doubter.[12]

Kierkegaard then spoke of his own difficulties with this varied complex of problems that was the focus of his enthusiastic interest. He felt like Hercules at the crossroads: "It is perhaps a misfortune of my existence that I am interested in all too many things, and not decisively in any one thing. My interests are not all subordinated under one heading, but are all coordinated with one another." He continued with lengthy reflections on the natural sciences, which attracted him, and on theology, which repelled him.

Kierkegaard wrote the second of these letters out in the country a month later, on July 6, 1835. Addressed to his friend P. E. Lind, this letter speaks of Kierkegaard's need to attend to his individuality:

> I do not deny that it betrays weakness and that it would be a sign of greater strength to have the ability, like many fish, to remain at the bottom of the sea without feeling the need to play frequently on the surface like the silver-glinting sunfish. Nor do I believe that I am so weak that I would simply perish if that element were denied me. . . . But on the one hand, just as I believe that such external circumstances could be advantageous for many and that in this case they have been advantageous for me, so, on the other hand, these circumstances can also promote the growth of an excess of tendrils and growths on the tree of life. This is because the sorts of people who have greatest need of this sort of external encouragement are precisely those who do not find inscribed within themselves the path they must take . . . but have to labor through life's dialectic in order to come to clarity about their destiny. . . . This situation is helpful to me insofar as it teaches me to focus my attention on my own inner self. It encourages me to grasp myself, my own self, and to cling firmly to it amid the infinite mutability of life. It incites me to seize hold of that concave mirror in which I have tried until now to view the life around me. . . . This pleases me because I see that I am able to do it, because I feel that I have the strength to hold the mirror, whether it shows me my ideal or my caricature, those two extremes between which life constantly oscillates, as H. Steffens says.[13]

The two passages cited above give a clear and quite detailed profile of the young Kierkegaard in the middle of his aesthetic period, when he had found the path that would lead him to his life's work. And here, once again, the background is Steffens and his *Caricatures of What Is Most Holy*. Kierkegaard read Steffens's book as he read most books, quite oblivious of the book's intentions but with an eye to how it could serve his own self-understanding or some item of particular interest — in this case, the anonymous intellectual life of the common people, both in the myths and mythology of the prehistoric era and in the fairy tales and folk songs of historical times.

Kierkegaard probably understood that it had been a daring and polemical act for Steffens to publish the book when he did, in 1819-21. For Germany, these years in the wake of the Napoleonic wars were turbulent ones, characterized by the rise of nationalism and reaction against the Congress of Vienna. In his work Steffens lashed out to the right and to the left, noting the incongruence between the demand of the ideal and its caricature in actuality. "Steffens has stuck his hand in a wasps' nest," Schelling[14] wrote. On the one hand, it was an attack, in the name of the new spirit of freedom, upon the indolent, self-satisfied mediocrity and cautious calm of the bourgeoisie. But on the other hand, French liberal ideas would have put a stop to the rise of German national consciousness, so Steffens adopted a reactionary stance against them. He took up arms against an abstract equality at odds with reality: the state was founded on the basis of the estates, with their differences and particularities. But Steffens also demanded freedom for the young and uniform schooling for both country and city, for the highborn and the lowly, and he attacked the popular *Turnverein* movement of Father Jahn.[15] All this cost Steffens his popularity and put him in danger of losing his position. Many of his friends turned away from him, and the rest failed to defend him. By publishing his simultaneously radical and reactionary views, Steffens produced confusion and indignation on all sides. He wrote to Schleiermacher: "A great mass of lies, deceptions, gossip, and meanness of all sorts has been directed against me. I have not detected a single appropriate comment. And what is worst is that my friends have disappeared so completely into the horde of abusers that with the best will in the world I am unable to say where utter vileness leaves off and callous friendship begins." This heated language was very close to that of Kierkegaard after his challenge to *The Corsair,* when he was faced with the task of writing about his own times' caricature of what was most holy.

Kierkegaard also thought of Steffens's book when he wrote his dissertation on Socrates and needed to define Plato's relation to myth: "Steffens's preface to *Caricatures of What Is Most Holy* is one such splendid depiction, in which the existence of Nature becomes a myth about the existence of Spirit." Like Steffens, Kierkegaard reflected upon the spontaneous imagery of myth that overwhelms the individual, who then loses his or her freedom because this sort of image is not freely produced or artfully created. It becomes impossible for reflective thought

> to differentiate the whole from itself and cause it to appear, light and volatile, in the sphere of pure poetry. This shows how the mythical can also assert itself in an isolated individual. The prototype of this must of course have had its effect on the development of nations. But one must bear in mind that it remains a myth only as long as it is repeated in the consciousness of nations, which in dreaming reproduce the myth of their past. Every attempt to treat myth historically demonstrates *ipso facto* that reflection has awakened and is killing the myth. Like the fairy tale, myth only holds sway in the twilight of the imagination. . . .[16]

The last seven or eight lines have nothing to do with Kierkegaard's dissertation, but are typical of his associative way of thinking. They are borrowed from Steffens's work and put into Kierkegaard's language. After this digression, he returned to Plato and myth. We have not yet seen anything of the common man or the simple person but, with Steffens as a connecting link, we have been on our way toward the simpler times that are older and deeper than history. According to the Romantics, this simpler era was nothing imperfect or amateurish, but was the source from which we could recover what had been destroyed by reflection and speculation.

When Kierkegaard traveled to Berlin in 1841, one of his purposes was of course to hear the renowned Steffens, who had himself become a kind of myth for the previous generation, which he had awakened at the dawn of the century. But Kierkegaard's great expectations met with disappointment. Steffens had always been broad and diffuse; now he was sixty-eight years old, and more diffuse than ever. His youthful enthusiasm had become an inexhaustible buoyancy. Kierkegaard wrote to Johannes Spang,[17] "The streets are too broad for me and so are Steffens's lectures. One cannot see from the one side to the other; one cannot keep track of the passersby, just as with Steffens's lectures."[18]

Kierkegaard wrote in more detail to Frederik Christian Sibbern:

I have heard Steffens several times . . . but strangely enough, he does not appeal to me at all. And I, who have read with such enormous enthusiasm much of what he has written, e.g., *Caricatures of What Is Most Holy,* just to mention one work; I, who had very much looked forward to hearing him in order to ascertain for myself what is generally said about him, that he is peerless as a lecturer: I am utterly disappointed. His lectures seem to me so uncertain and so full of hesitations that you doubt that you are getting anywhere. And when he is transfigured by a flash of genius, I miss the artistic awareness, the oratorical superiority I have so often admired in his writings. . . . Therefore I prefer to read him. His *Anthropology* is of course rather difficult reading for anyone who is not well versed in the natural sciences. Incidentally, it has been quite painful for me to find myself disappointed in this respect. This is why I did not call on him, either. On the whole, I live as isolated as possible and am withdrawing more and more into myself.[19]

It is not known what Sibbern wrote in reply, but he may well have been reminded of his own sojourn in Germany thirty years earlier, when he heard Steffens in Breslau and wrote home to Sophie Ørsted, "I have found no one on my journey whose personal presence is so instructive and refreshing to the heart as his,"[20] and "I will always cherish the hours I spent in Breslau with Steffens."[21]

But despite his disappointment over his failure to experience the fireworks that had been spoken of so often by Sibbern and the older generation when they recalled Steffens as a twenty-nine-year-old lecturer at Eler's Hall, Kierkegaard's devotion to Steffens's work remained unshaken. He continued to read Steffens both for inspiration and for confirmation of his own thoughts. In Steffens he saw clearly the tension between speculation, on the one hand, and the emphasis on the individual and the existential, on the other — the tension that had made so great an impression on Sibbern and on Poul Martin Møller. And Kierkegaard also understood that there still remained something of the Schellingian school in Steffens, despite Steffens's break with the speculative attempt to reveal the innermost secret of life, and despite his having written *On False Theology and True Faith* (1823), in which he proclaimed his adherence to old-fashioned

Lutheranism. There is a lengthy account of this in Kierkegaard's papers from 1847, when he was sharpening his religious categories in the wake of his battle with *The Corsair*. "Henrich Steffens," he wrote,

> is a good example of how a well-meaning orthodoxy — which does not shrink from asserting that if the least little bit in Christianity can be subjected to the corrective of thinking (in the sense that thinking is to decide things), then everything is lost — ends, nonetheless, in confusion. In his *Philosophy of Religion*[22] . . . he shows that miracles are an obstacle to thinking. If thinking is to be permitted to decide about something because it cannot grasp it, then Christianity is lost. So what does Steffens do? He produces a theory which, *thinking,* finds it quite proper that miracles are included. Alas, alas, alas. . . . Christianity is related neither to thinking nor to doubt, but to will and to *obedience:* thou shalt believe. This wanting to include thinking is disobedience, regardless of whether it says Yes or No.[23]

But otherwise Kierkegaard had a very high opinion of Steffens's work on the philosophy of religion. Just a few days after the above entry, on October 3, 1847, Kierkegaard cited Steffens's work again because it contained a remark that confirmed his vision of the relation between the individual and the crowd: "Henrich Steffens's *Philosophy of Religion*[24] thus speaks the terrifying certainty that with respect to the internal in history, the crowd means evil." Kierkegaard went on to cite another trenchant remark that occurs a couple of pages later in Steffens's book: "The Savior died for the entire world, but is resurrected only for true Christians."[25]

In 1848 Kierkegaard returned to Steffens's *Philosophy of Religion* again, but in his haste he remembered incorrectly and referred to Steffens's *Anthropology.* Here we have echoes from the battle with *The Corsair:* "The ungodliness of people, wherein they have taught one another how to be released from having to do the Good (indeed, have put Evil — selfishness — in the place of the Good) has precisely the result that the person who wishes once again to express the Good must come to suffer. In order to express the standard of measure, he must suffer — and consequently does suffer for the sins of the others."[26]

In Kierkegaard's *The Concept of Anxiety* (1844) we see the decisive importance of Steffens's work. Kierkegaard referred to Steffens in the draft, but in the work as published he referred to the school of Schelling. He mentioned Schelling's lectures on Böhme: "This sort of thing must always be used with suspicion."[27] On the other hand, as Torsten Bohlin has demonstrated,[28] Kierkegaard found in Steffens's book on the philosophy of religion a confirmation of his fundamental idea that anxiety was simultaneously attractive and repugnant. Indeed, at a number of points Steffens anticipated the intention of Kierkegaard's book. In the section on objective anxiety, Kierkegaard wrote that "certain men of the Schellingian school have been especially careful to note the alteration that sin occasions in the creature," which is in fact the expression of objective anxiety. In his footnote concerning the word "alteration," we see a typical example of Kierkegaard's associative way of thinking:

> The [Danish] word "alteration" expresses the ambiguity very well. The word "alter" [*alterere*] is indeed used in the sense of transforming, distorting, or removing something from its original state (the thing becomes something else). But one also says "to become altered" [*at blive altereret*] in the sense of becoming terrified. . . . With us [in Danish] the word is usually employed in everyday speech only in the sense of being terrified, and thus one generally hears the common man say, "I was quite altered" [*altereret*]. At least I have heard a woman street-peddler say it.[29]

It was precisely the ambiguity inherent in the word that permitted Kierkegaard to use humor to criticize the thoughtless way the Schellingian school (though not Steffens) treated natural anxiety. This is not the place to sort out this argument; the point here is merely to establish that Steffens not only opened the way to myth and mythology but also inspired and confirmed the central feature of Kierkegaard's work — namely, religious thought.

Like Poul Martin Møller, Steffens, another widely traveled expatriate Dane, was among Kierkegaard's guides and benefactors during the difficult years of his youth. As we have noted, Kierkegaard could certainly be critical of Steffens, and he became suspicious when he saw speculation attempting in any way to define Christianity. But throughout his life, Kierkegaard felt a fellowship with this poet-philosopher who, although he had been caught up in the waves of Romanticism, strenuously denied that they could carry him to Heaven — or, to use Kierkegaard's words, "into the embrace of Eternity." It was Steffens's sense of reality, his view of the individual, of the existential, that led him away from the quasi-religious trance of speculation to a firm basis in old-fashioned Lutheranism.

Finally, we should also remember Steffens's significance for Grundtvig, for whom Steffens was both the man who opened up the portals to the world of mythology and the author of *On False Theology and True Faith*. That work was translated into Danish in 1825 and was warmly reviewed by Grundtvig, for whom it served as part of the inspiration for *The Church's Reply* (1825).[30] But Steffens was especially important to Grundtvig as an awakener and a prophet who cut right through all philosophy and went straight to existential issues, to the question of choice, to the matter of taking a position, of making a decision. This was the germ of the idea of the folk high school, an idea initially broached by Grundtvig and subsequently put into practice by Christen Kold[31] (more in the spirit of Kierkegaard than of Grundtvig), an idea that served as a source of awakening and enlightenment for the common man.

CHAPTER THREE

The Shadow of Jacob Christian Lindberg

The problem of internal self-definition, which we have examined as a
philosophical issue in the previous chapters, was Kierkegaard's principal interest. He linked it to the question of equality. The question of
equality, in turn, had its roots in the tangled web of problems that constituted Romanticism, but it also had a lineage that ran through the work of
Johann von Herder (Romantically interpreted) and on into the anonymous spiritual life of the common people as expressed in mythology, legend, and folk songs.

But at the dawn of the century, around the time of Henrich Steffens's
lectures in Copenhagen, self-definition had taken on decisive significance
for the common man in Denmark in a way that transcended philosophy.
The issue was in the times and in the air, so to speak, but it also had particular connections with the Danish peasant reforms and with French Revolutionary notions of freedom and equality. The spread of Romantic ideas
also helped to foster a climate that, however unconsciously, favored internal development in defiance of all external authority, especially in matters
concerning religion.

These factors came together in the so-called religious awakenings that
recent historiography has given credit for having formed the basis for the
religious, social, and political development of modern Denmark. Even if
we take into account the preparatory role played by the *Herrnhut* or
Moravian movement, this national uprising against the class of clerics and
government officials (those whom Kierkegaard called the "cultivated")

seems to have been spontaneous. Pietism and theological rationalism had been upper-class movements, and by and large they had not had much effect on the common people, who merely followed along and did not speculate much about the changing fashions in preaching the gospel. Both pietism and rationalism had been officially authorized. The religious awakenings surely came about as a result of the fact that, beneath the various strains of official orthodoxy, pietism, and rationalism, an old-fashioned Lutheranism still survived. This religiosity broke through and confirmed the common man in his awakening sense of his capacity for internal self-definition. It gave him the courage to break away from (or take an independent view of) the state-authorized understanding of Christianity, which in most cases was still official rationalism. In various groups and gatherings, in cells that soon appeared in almost every parish of the land, common people took matters pertaining to their salvation into their own hands. At the height of the awakenings, the principal devotional book was Luther's *Postil,* translated by Jørgen Thisted in 1825. This *Postil* was an important work in Kierkegaard's own collection of devotional literature. By and large, Kierkegaard did not know much of Luther apart from this volume, which he refers to most frequently in his papers.

The religious awakenings were marked by a mixture of reaction (i.e., back to true Lutheranism) and revolution (i.e., the battle against the power of the clergy, both in their role of proclaiming the gospel and as representatives of the ruling class in society). The awakenings were prosecuted on the basis of a 1741 law against assemblies and were punished both with fines and with imprisonment, which only served to accelerate the movement's growth and strengthen its internal solidarity. The authorities suspected, quite rightly, that behind the religious issue there was a social and political agenda, namely the common man's assertion of independence and authority in areas quite other than religion. The whole of official Denmark (including N. F. S. Grundtvig) viewed this springtime of the common people with skepticism.

Only one man understood its true significance: Jacob Christian Lindberg[1] — and perhaps also his silent observer, the young Søren Kierkegaard. We know of Kierkegaard's admiration for Lindberg from the polemic against Grundtvig in the *Concluding Unscientific Postscript.* We know that Lindberg was a frequent caller at the Kierkegaard family home on Nytorv[2] as a friend of Kierkegaard's older brother, who was himself a participant in the notorious gatherings in Lindberg's home. So Kierkegaard must have known quite a bit about Lindberg's struggle, his difficulties, and his sufferings. Kierkegaard was a reader of the *Scandinavian Church Times,* in which Lindberg carried out his furious struggle against the persecutors of the revival movement, and he was also familiar with Lindberg's polemical pieces and theological works.[3] But he does not say anything about the struggle itself, which was just ebbing out in 1832, when Kierkegaard was nineteen years old. Furthermore, Lindberg was affiliated with Grundtvig and his ecclesiastical views, which (at first, instinctively) were not to Kierkegaard's taste. But except for Jakob Peter Mynster,[4] Poul Martin Møller, and Steffens, Kierkegaard nowhere expressed such great and unreserved admiration for anyone as he did for Lindberg. When polemicizing against Grundtvig in the *Postscript,* he also took the occasion to defend Lindberg against the prevailing view of the times, which held him to be a sophist. This was a daring difference of opinion with the decided majority of the cultured elite, who saw in the learned Magister Lindberg only a quarrelsome troublemaker:

> I have never been able to detect anything sophistical in Lindberg's actions, if, as is only just and reasonable, I refuse to presume myself inspired to pass judgment upon what is in the hearts of others — and Lindberg has continually been persecuted on the basis of this sort of judgment. . . . As for Magister Lindberg, he is a man of so many excellent abilities and is so experienced a dialectician that he is a great help as an ally, and as a foe he can always make things difficult for an opponent in battle.[5]

Kierkegaard went on to emphasize Lindberg's merits at Grundtvig's expense. Kierkegaard had a stubborn distaste for Grundtvig (as he did for Hans Christian Andersen).[6] His distaste was rooted less in substantive differences, however much he tried to specify them, than in differences of temperament, and in the cases of both men this distaste caused Kierkegaard's arguments to miss their mark. Although he may have been right in

21

the individual points he emphasized, those points were of course far from being the whole story. Thus Kierkegaard could acknowledge that Grundtvig had an explosive sort of genius, but this is scarcely the whole truth, and particularly not when it is put forward by someone like Kierkegaard, who wanted to present himself as a dialectician. But in his comparison of Grundtvig and Lindberg, Kierkegaard did not really grasp the latter's position in church politics.

Lindberg's stand was not only a campaign against the rationalists and a defense of those participating in the religious awakenings; in the final analysis it was also a campaign against the awakeners' own nascent tendencies toward sectarianism, free churches, and opposition to the state church. And it was here that Lindberg turned to Grundtvig's view of the church: (1) as relying on the Apostles' Creed as the gospel in miniature, which prevents people from forming sects on the basis of arbitrary interpretations of the Bible, and (2) as a counterweight to free church tendencies, the release of people from the legal restrictions that compelled them to worship only in the parish in which they resided. But we cannot expect Kierkegaard to have understood the church-political situation in which Lindberg found himself when he occupied his dangerous strategic position, where he alone held all the strands in his hands and could easily have led the people of the religious assemblies in an exodus from the narrow dogmatic and juridical confines of the state church. Lindberg alone had an overview of the entire situation. His alliance with Grundtvig was more a product of his tactical view of church politics in the immediate situation than of theological considerations, even though he did come close to Grundtvig's position in theology as well, albeit in his own way — quite like Peter Christian Kierkegaard.[7] In these cases, one cannot speak of disciple relationships such as those involving Grundtvig's faithful band of clerical friends.

In his later years Kierkegaard would renew Lindberg's campaign in the name of the common man against a church staffed by civil servants. Kierkegaard's tactic would be to demonstrate, indirectly, to the cultivated world what Christianity was and to "breathe inwardness into the Establishment." But despite this, we cannot expect Kierkegaard, either as a young man or later on, to have understood the church-political actions of

Lindberg and Grundtvig, whose intention was to create a broad framework within which the Christianity of the "awakened" common man could exist. Kierkegaard never came to a full understanding of Grundtvig, although to have done so was not beyond the realm of possibility. Therefore, Kierkegaard's argument in the *Concluding Unscientific Postscript* against Grundtvig's ecclesiastical views was rather thin and unsatisfactory. Kierkegaard's critique of Grundtvig was not based on a study of the latter's writings; he owned only a couple of Grundtvig's works and, with the exception of *Braga Talk*[8] (1844), little or nothing from after 1837, when the first part of the *Hymns* appeared. Kierkegaard owned Grundtvig's *Overview of World History* from 1817, the *Sermons or Sunday Book* from 1827-30, the two volumes of mythology (1808 and 1832), *Danish Proverbs and Sayings* (1845), and finally, *A Little Bible Chronicle for Children and the Common Man* from 1814. Kierkegaard's understanding of the debate about Grundtvig's view of the church was not based on a study of Grundtvig but on several lectures Lindberg gave at the University in 1835. Kierkegaard summarized them in his journals,[9] and it is these journal entries that he polemically recast in the *Postscript*.

On the street Kierkegaard maintained a "jovial relationship" with Grundtvig, and they discussed, among other things, his strained relationship to Mynster. But in his journals Kierkegaard was constantly sarcastic toward Grundtvig and his popular and patriotic actions of the 1840s (such as his speeches at the nationalist meetings on Skamlingsbank), his world-historical visions, and much more.

Kierkegaard's entire critique of Grundtvig, however, rested on a flimsy foundation and was based on an emotional reaction to the overwhelming bombast and fecundity of Grundtvig's personality, which prevented Kierkegaard from appreciating their shared antipathy to late Romanticism and its ideal of cultivation, as well as to leveling and to reflectiveness. Both Kierkegaard and Grundtvig were firmly grounded in the principle of contradiction. That principle formed the basis for Grundtvig's attack, in his polemical *World History* (1812), upon the whole of Schellingian Romantic speculation. This work was also Grundtvig's attack on objective systems, and it was just as trenchant, though not as philosophically subtle, as Kierkegaard's attack in the *Concluding Unscientific Postscript*. Both opposed the religiously tinged individualism and subjectivism of their times, which sometimes employed Christian rhetoric as a cover for a spiritual humanism and other times converted the Christian standpoint and its requirements into magic and cults. In the *Concluding Unscientific Postscript* and in his book on Adler, Kierkegaard attacked the idea that subjectivism is a psychological category. Grundtvig did the same thing in his important essay *On True Christianity* (1826), where he opposed those who define Christianity on the basis of a need for religion that, unburdened by the requirements of the gospel, led people "down deplorable blind alleys, [so that] they created for themselves a heathen mythology that has the appearance of Christianity, or (to use the customary language of church history) they lost themselves in unreasoning fanaticism and in mystical figments of their imagination."[10] For both Kierkegaard and Grundtvig, the Romantic period's danger lay precisely in its fascination with an indefinable "higher" something — in other words, the danger was Romanticism's religiosity. This is what Kierkegaard targeted in his book on Adler, where he wrote that "One does not become a Christian by being religiously seized by something higher, and not every outpouring of religious emotion is a Christian outpouring."[11] Grundtvig, who had not been confused by the overwrought religiosity of Romanticism since his break with it in 1810, heartily concurred with Kierkegaard on this point.

There were other similarities as well. Both Kierkegaard and Grundtvig opposed the nascent liberalism of the 1840s. Both were caricatured and hounded by *The Corsair* and made to appear ridiculous to cultivated Copenhagen. Grundtvig had never belonged to high society, so the coteries that determined the taste and fashion of the times did not take him especially seriously. By contrast, cultivated Copenhagen never forgave Kierkegaard, whom they viewed as one of their own, even though they always suspected that the hosier's son harbored a dangerous tendency toward rebellion. And finally, the two men shared an interest in the question of the common man, of the ordinary, simple people, who were still waiting patiently out in the hall, in the antechambers, but among whom there was a certain revolt in progress, a revolt that was understood and supported by the same Lindberg who was a friend both of Grundtvig and of Kierkegaard. Naturally, each saw the problem in his own way. It would be too much to attempt to sort out the nuances here, but in brief, both men saw the hope of the future in the common man. For Kierkegaard, this hope was to be understood in the specifically religious sense. For Grundtvig, it was to be understood across a broad religious, social, and national front as the common folk on the way to becoming a people.

Both men were interested in the cause of the common man, but it was Kierkegaard who in fact had more direct contact with ordinary people. Proclaiming that "everything must now be of the people," Grundtvig allowed his visions and songs about the common people to obscure their actual existence and destiny. Kierkegaard, on the other hand, was unable to entertain such a category as "folkishness" [*Folkelighed*]. He bridled every time he suspected the presence of the crowd, and he made it a firm point of his philosophy that, from a religious point of view, the crowd meant untruth, except insofar as each person in the crowd, separately and as a single individual, appropriated a shared idea and related himself or herself to that idea. In that case he could praise revolution, as he did in *A Literary Review,* though only as an event of transient significance.[12] If the shared idea had to do with eternity, and if the crowd thus became a *congregation,* matters immediately became more difficult for Kierkegaard.

But in practice Kierkegaard was more a man of the people than the lonely and often inaccessible Grundtvig. As we will see, Kierkegaard had a particular talent for contact with people, a talent based on shared understanding, which stemmed in part from his capacity to see his father and mother behind the ordinary men and women he met and dealt with — never condescending from on high, never with self-important reserve, but cordially and straightforwardly. In his journals Kierkegaard wrote repeatedly that *humanity* [*Menneskelighed*] is *human equality* [*Menneske-Lighed*]. As always, both in his external behavior and in his internal reflections, the gospel also played a role: blessed are the simple. Kierkegaard, for whom understanding followed by action was everything, felt himself obligated in this respect, and also humbled by the meager imitation of Christ he was able to manage with respect to common people.

Similarly, the poor always had access to Kierkegaard's otherwise inaccessible home. Nevertheless, despite what some well-to-do pharisaical snoopers into his financial affairs might believe to be the duties of someone truly holy, Kierkegaard did not give his fortune away, and he repeatedly insisted that he not be regarded as a saint or as an apostle with authority. Like most people, he gave without reflecting upon private property, capitalism, and social problems. But to the money he gave he added the mercy that transforms alms into a gift, that constitutes a gift behind the gift, without which a gift loses all its ethical significance, becoming perhaps nothing more than an attempt to salve a bad social conscience rather than what Kierkegaard called a "work of love" in his great book of the same name. In this aspect of his life, too, the gospel was present: "I will leave you, but the poor you will always have with you." Kierkegaard saw in the poor a representative of the Christ who had no place to lay his head. His papers contain a little passage which, because of its personal reference, he did not include in "Guilty–Not Guilty":

> How much is written about compassion toward those in need, how many examples are given, how often it is mentioned in the newspapers. And yet the best thing about it, the most endearing, the little psychological trait that gives the gift infinite worth, the trait that, if it is absent, turns the sum of money into jingling coins, is never described. I knew a man who himself lived in straitened circumstances, who did not have a great deal to give away, and whose name was never mentioned. . . . [Y]et I learned more from him than from all the stories in the newspapers. Sometimes he gave to a poor person on the street, but when he gave he concealed it as much as possible, and he always removed his hat with as much respect for the poor person as if that person were his superior, and with as much friendliness as if that person were his equal.[13]

Here we see Kierkegaard in a personal moment, the sort of situation that he usually concealed. This is just the sort of situation where many people, waving a copy of the New Testament (of which they are otherwise ignorant), would insist upon a quite different sort of imitation without considering making a humiliating admission of their own shortcomings.

CHAPTER FOUR

The Home on Nytorv and the Religious Awakening Movement

B y 1830, the religious awakenings had focused attention on the life and culture of the common people. Jacob Christian Lindberg's struggle personified this issue, and N. F. S. Grundtvig also involved himself with it from a distance. The common people naturally became a topic of lively interest in the Nytorv home of Michael Pedersen Kierkegaard,[1] particularly for the old man himself and for his son Peter Christian. The latter had received his theological degree at the age of twenty-one, studied abroad for a number of years, earned a doctorate from Göttingen, and returned home to Denmark in 1830 with doubts and anxieties about the future. At that time, Søren had just become a university student and as such had been enrolled in the Royal Guard, but was discharged several days later as unfit for service. He was now a theological student but devoted most of his energies to aesthetics, coming to grips with himself, and enjoying himself with his friends. Even with his conflicting feelings of piety and contentiousness, Søren was a ferocious dialectician. He was both melancholic and exultant, as gifted young people often are at that age.

During the 1830s, it was in the family home on Nytorv that Søren experienced not only his own inner conflicts but also the external conflicts of the times. In the Kierkegaard home the issues of the day were the standing topic of debate among a group including Søren's father, his brother, and their friends, most of whom had ties to Grundtvig and Lindberg, both of whom frequented the place. The house on Nytorv was something of a cultural center in Copenhagen at the time, and the primary topics of debate were questions concerning the common people. It seems unlikely that Søren participated in these debates to any extent, but he was an avid listener and was particularly impressed by Lindberg's superiority as a debater, as well as by his own father. In these conversations the elder Kierkegaard was often torn between Jakob Peter Mynster, who had been the object of his devotion for many years, and the young Grundtvigians and Lindberg, who pulled in the opposite direction on the question of the religious awakenings. Lindberg held the old man's attention fully as much as did the august bishop, whom he received with reverence.

Mynster, in turn, treated the old hosier with friendliness, but without much understanding of what was stirring in him — an obliviousness that the old man probably noticed. This dynamic did not escape Søren's astute gaze, even though he only mentioned it twenty years later: "Then Father died. I myself was the one who brought word to Mynster. His response at the time contrasted curiously with his words six years later about how well he could remember Father, words which he even published in an attempt to please me."[2] He didn't repeat what Mynster said, but it was certainly something of a generally comforting and patronizing nature, without any clear recollection of the old man. The article that Mynster published in Heiberg's *Intelligencer* in order to flatter Søren contains the following lines: "I find it quite moving that Magister Kierkegaard continues to dedicate his edifying discourses to his father's memory. For I, too, knew that honorable man. He was a straightforward citizen; he went through life with an open mind; he had never immersed himself in any philosophy. How, then, can it be that his son, with all his fine education, continually thinks of this man, who has long since gone to his rest?"[3] Mynster, then, apparently understood nothing of the Kierkegaard family. He didn't understand the father, who had in fact immersed himself quite thoroughly in philosophy and theology. Nor did he understand the son, his filial piety, or the reasons why he dedicated his works (not without ulterior motives) to "My father, former hosier" — who was otherwise known and respected in the city as the wealthy merchant Kierkegaard in the big house on Nytorv. Even Georg Brandes apparently allowed himself to be misled: "In Kierkegaard's writings we encounter a whiff of the stuffy atmosphere of the hosiery shop."[4]

Nevertheless, the elder Kierkegaard held Mynster in esteem. He par-

ticularly honored Mynster as the young curate who had come to Copenhagen in 1811 and in his own way had established a counterweight to the
rationalists, a counterweight Kierkegaard otherwise had sought in the
Moravian congregation on Stormgade.[5] There is a certain poetic emphasis
in Søren Kierkegaard's continuing mention of Mynster as "my father's
pastor," in which he ties his own loyalty to Mynster to that shown by his
father. But this can hardly be the whole truth; it is unlikely that Søren's father, who was a strong and fiercely independent person, had retained
much of the unquestioning and submissive respect for the clergy that often characterized those of lower station. Still, Mynster had been a central
figure in Michael Kierkegaard's life during difficult times: Mynster had
confirmed his sons and buried his wives — he had come to his home in
sorrow and in joy. Furthermore, Mynster's sermons always contained earnest words that helped the father, which he in turn recommended to his
sons, each of whom had his own weaknesses. The father himself was a
man of strength, "a man of enormous will," Søren wrote at one point. Under his calm exterior there were strong passions and a powerful imagination that, when controlled, gave warmth to his wit and sting to his irony:
"He was the most gifted person I have met," wrote his eldest son. Hans
Brøchner[6] and Frederik Hammerich,[7] both of whom were guests in the
house, made similar statements.

Writings on Michael Kierkegaard's relationship to his youngest son
could fill an entire library, but it has been extremely difficult to sort out
poetry from fact. The father was made of sterner stuff and had his concerns about his weaker youngest son. The old man, with all his strengths
— and weaknesses — loved Søren. His eldest son had something more
straightforward about him, and the old man was proud of him, but was
hardly close to him. Whatever the case, it was with his youngest son that
the elder Kierkegaard shared his innermost thoughts, his hopes and anxieties. And behind the patriarchal authority of his father, Søren could
glimpse a troubled human being — a Job, a Daniel in the lion's den. We do
not know a great deal, even though the published works and papers seem
to tell us almost too much. They always mix poetry and reality. Søren was
a thinker, but he was also a great poet and artist of fantasy. Even where he
confides in his diaries, it is only behind the scrim of poetry that we are able

to sense the faintest contours of his fiancée[8] and his father. Only the most naive devotees of psychology believe they can uncover the real truth about these relationships in Kierkegaard's works.

Søren probably did not understand his father fully, but in him he encountered spirit and instinct, repentance and faith, and anxiety and humor, about which he himself could reflect and wax poetic. In his father he encountered, almost palpably, a "common man" for whom education was neither a crutch nor a mask and for whom dialectics were not speculative fencing but expressions of existential conflicts and contradictions, saturated with the passion that made them into absolutes. Søren's relation to his father shattered any possible respect he might have had for the sort of education he saw among the upper-class elite, and the categories of the common man and the simple person became absolutely fundamental both to his philosophy and to his final actions. For Kierkegaard, of course, "simplicity" is not to be understood in the intellectual-psychological sense, but evangelically, concerning the pure of heart who shall see God through sin, doubt, and repentance.

The old man was firmly planted in the middle of life. Behind him lay his transformation from a poor shepherd boy into a wealthy merchant. Søren, on the other hand, was an outsider. With the support of the great fortune he inherited, his seismographic sensitivity and sense of fantasy enabled him to create, almost from thin air, the literary art that we today find more satisfying than that of his contemporaries, who required the assistance of mountains of tangible material in order to produce anything. It would be foolish to read Kierkegaard's writings literally in an attempt to discover the reality of his private life. He was a poet, and he would have been so to an even greater degree had not his father given him a cross to bear: "reality," the word that always called Søren back to earth from flights of poetry and the conjuring of illusion; "reality," whose categories — spirit, honesty, and rectitude — are concerned with the relation of existence to itself, concerned with the sickness unto death that prepares us for fundamental recovery. It would be shallow to think of a father fixation here. The true upbringing that takes place in any home is always the self-education of the parents, and what was of decisive importance in Søren's experience was his encounter with his father's self-education in everyday life, with the self-discipline that was the basis for the old man's authority and independence of spirit.

It is not my intention to analyze Kierkegaard's many statements about his father or the supposed reflection of the figure of his father in his poetic and philosophical writings. Rather, it is my intention to caution the psychologically curious about the dangers of reading Kierkegaard literally in order to divine whatever may be the private meanings of various secret notes, which (if I guess correctly) cannot provide any explanation whatever of Kierkegaard's writings. On the contrary, Kierkegaard's written work, in all its complexity, can be fully understood on the basis of the presuppositions contained in the texts themselves. The truth is that the father's triumph of self-discipline over his natural and instinctual life simply did not result in the creation of those complexes and neuroses that constitute psychology's all-too-simple explanations. On the contrary, the health of the human spirit is the fruit of an anxiety that neither enervates one nor leads one astray, but leads to rebirth, integrity, and the earnest reality of the self. This is what Kierkegaard never forgot when he thought of his father. That is why, in matters pertaining to the truth and the self, he always considered it wrong to treat subjectivity as a psychological category.

The task at hand is to define and describe the climate in Kierkegaard's home during his youth in the 1830s. Some details of his father's childhood are well known, including the occasion on which he cursed God, which he could never forget. In his remarks on this incident, the poet in Søren describes it in terms that probably do not correspond to reality. It is unlikely that Michael Kierkegaard was nerve-racked or plagued with scruples or haunted by this little reminiscence from his childhood (which we can interpret as a sign of his fervor and religious reflectiveness as a child) until the scourge of death came upon his home, claiming five of his children, his two wives, and his daughter-in-law. At that point he plunged into the religious brooding that dredged up this childhood memory and linked it to his obsessional notion of a just God who visits his vengeance upon those who sin against him. This was also when the old man's youth passed before him, filled with many hidden and half-forgotten episodes about which we can only speculate and which most probably constitute the kernel of his legendary "earthquake," his confession to his youngest son, who thus was made privy to the weakness, penitence, and guilt feelings harbored by his otherwise-strong father. We know nothing certain about all this except that it gave Søren a wealth of material to reflect upon and use as the stuff of fiction. We find echoes of it in *The Concept of Anxiety* and in the piece "'Guilty?'/'Not Guilty?'" in *Stages on Life's Way*. Above all, it was in this episode that Søren encountered the reality of religious experience: Christianity is a profound matter that encompasses the entire self, from the fall to the resurrection.

In Kierkegaard's later writings it is impossible to sort out the influence of his father's religious experience from the influence of his own. In his writings he allowed his own Christianity to remain undefined. For the good of his cause Kierkegaard liked to say (with polemical intent) that he was not a Christian, but that he knew what Christianity was. He said this toward the end of his life, when he envisioned such high requirements of Christianity that human beings could not meet them but were compelled to break down and acknowledge their inadequacy. There can be no doubt that Kierkegaard's father was the existential foundation of such a stance. Similarly, Kierkegaard's father's influence was obvious in the willful one-sidedness with which his son embraced the New Testament command to imitate Christ and in his son's vision of the humiliated Christ, the Good Friday scene — while speaking only rarely of Easter and having no use either for Pentecost or Christmas (Kierkegaard only mentioned Pentecost once, in the sermon in *For Self-Examination*). Like Luther, Kierkegaard believed himself to be a corrective to established Christianity, a task which for Kierkegaard, as for Luther, meant the "introduction of Christianity into Christendom." An emphasis on the degraded Christ, Good Friday, and the imitation of Christ was fundamental for Kierkegaard. Only after understanding these notions in all their strictness and inescapability could one speak of Easter and Pentecost, and only then could grace become a reality — not after an easy escape from imitating Christ by the acknowledgement of one's weakness.

This was quite clearly Kierkegaard's father's understanding of Christianity, and it fit well with the Moravianism with which his father had been acquainted from his childhood home and which he subsequently sought out in Copenhagen. Although he never explicitly joined the Society of

Brothers, Michael Kierkegaard was always among the listeners at the Sunday evening gatherings in Stormgade and was a member of the governing committee until his death — this despite the fact that he was also a member of the state church and Mynster was his pastor. And Mynster notwithstanding, it was certainly in Stormgade that the elder Kierkegaard acquired his view of Christianity, focusing upon what the Congregation of Brothers called "the Man of Pain" — the degraded Christ with his blood and wounds — and upon the inward conviction necessary for devotion to him. Both Peter Christian and Søren were taken to these meetings as children. (Other participants included the Brandt,[9] Hammerich, and Boesen[10] families, as well as Councillor Olsen, the father of Regine.) It was here that both sons saw emphasized that aspect of Christianity that, with their father in mind, they themselves would subsequently stress in their preaching and philosophy. It was here that Søren first experienced the awakening movement, in a discreet and undemonstrative form. It was here that he saw the common people come in throngs — naturally, of course, after they had attended the obligatory service in their parish churches in the morning.

In the rural districts of Søren's father's childhood, religious life had been awakened by the traveling Moravian pastors Gert Hansen and Bloch, who started a movement that subsequently found a center in Stauning, about five miles from Sædding, where the Moravian sympathizer Jens Bering was pastor of the local church.[11] In other respects, the Kierkegaard family home was steeped in the sturdy faith of the common people, containing elements of fatalism and especially a belief in Providence, which discerned signs and messages from God in chance events. This belief was also something typical of Michael Kierkegaard's two sons, particularly Peter Christian, who heeded omens in dreams and discerned the hand of God in the most random events. But Søren, too, could often be surprised at how the gospel reading of the day accorded with a present situation. He could go to Mynster or Madvig to discuss an appointment at the pastoral seminary, find no one at home, and take it as a sign of Providence. It is in this context that we are to understand the family conviction that none of the children would survive his or her thirty-fourth year, the age at which Jesus died — while the father, as a sort of punishment, would survive them all. This conviction is only one of many examples of how the beliefs of common people, including an everyday faith in Providence, had deep roots in the Kierkegaard family.

Despite its extensive missionary activity, Moravianism never really found a firm foothold in Denmark. While it could certainly nourish people's spirits by encouraging the inward appropriation of faith, and many certainly preferred it to rationalistic sermonizing, there was something quietistic, even cowardly, about Moravianism. If a state-church pastor would surprise a meeting in progress, the Moravian missionary would disappear out the door. When the religious awakening came, this aspect of Moravianism became more apparent, and people turned away from it because they found it wanting in readiness to suffer for the faith — this quite apart from the Lutheran criticism of the movement's one-sidedness.

Despite Mynster's influence, Søren Kierkegaard never completely abandoned the Moravian climate of his childhood home, but he rarely mentioned the movement. Only at one point in 1850 did he refer to the Moravians even briefly: "The Congregation of Brothers does not emphasize imitation; instead of the lyricism of the blood-theory [that is, the standard theological view of Christ's blood as sacrificial atonement] there is all this gawking at Christ's sufferings."[12] This was precisely the view held by the people involved in the peasant religious movement. But Peter Larsen Skræppenborg[13] was right when he asked the members of his assembly not to be too hard on the Moravians, to whom he owed his own awakening. The Moravians could be credited with an appeal to inwardness, to reflection and appropriation, regardless of whether one shared the Moravians' particular doctrinal views. The life of the religious awakenings in Copenhagen (and this includes the climate in the Kierkegaard family home on Nytorv) cannot be understood apart from the background of the Moravian Sunday meetings in the assembly hall on Stormgade. Bethesda and the Grundtvigian center, now Vartov,[14] which constituted the two focal points of the fourth and fifth generations of the awakening movement, are directly descended from the Moravians of Stormgade.

The Congregation of Brothers was founded in 1739 and was organized in accordance with the Moravian pattern. Shortly thereafter came the anti-conventicle law of 1741, which shattered the organization, but small groups maintained connections with Moravian-minded pastors, such as

Pastor Lemming of Nikolai Church, who confirmed Michael Pedersen Kierkegaard in 1773. The following year, the no less Moravian-minded Peter Saxtorp became curate and moved in next door to M. P. Kierkegaard's uncle, Niels Seding, in whose home Michael Pedersen was raised. Saxtorp was Seding's pastor and was a regular visitor in his home. Thus there was an unbroken connection with the religious awakening movement of the faraway West Jutland village of M. P. Kierkegaard's childhood.

The Congregation of Brothers steered a careful course within the conditions laid down by the anti-conventicle law. Since the members acknowledged membership in the established church, which thus performed the official ecclesiastical ceremonies (baptism, confirmation, administration of the sacrament, and burial), they were permitted to erect a building for their edifying meetings: their well-known meeting hall in Stormgade. Attendance at the Sunday evening meetings varied, but around 1815 it increased sharply, in part because of religious stirrings among the Copenhagen middle class (historians influenced by Marxism will certainly note the state bankruptcy of 1813 in this connection) and in part because Johannes Christian Reuss became head of the congregation, as well as the fact that the Sunday evening meetings were now open to the public. Although they did not make the point too sharply, the Congregation of Brothers represented an evangelical reaction against the predominantly rationalistic clergy of Copenhagen.

It should also be remembered that in 1811 Mynster had entered the picture as an impassioned young curate at the Church of Our Lady. (That church was being rebuilt after its destruction by fire, so Mynster's congregation actually met in Trinity Church.) Similar attacks on rationalism issued from Mynster's pulpit. Mynster was particularly effective among the upper-middle class and especially among cultivated people, who found the aesthetic side of his preaching to their taste. Mynster's message was in fact less an attack than an attempt to give substance and dogmatic structure to the dominant rationalism. Even in these early sermons, one can discern Mynster's peculiar gifts as a communicator and his flexibility and adaptability. He was attacked both by the more heavy-handed rationalists and by some from the Moravian-pietist circle. Nonetheless, it cannot be denied that Mynster's pulpit was the beginning point for a new era in the ecclesiastical history of Copenhagen — even though, despite Mynster's increasingly dominant position, the religious depths of his preaching ran a bit shallower than might have been expected. Søren Kierkegaard was to struggle with this dilemma throughout his life, until he concluded on his deathbed that Mynster had been "a poisonous plant."[15]

But the subterranean unrest in Copenhagen, which paralleled developments in the religious awakenings all over the country, was of decisive significance. It was precisely this unrest, this internal crisis of the self, that had been awakened and called to arms, but had not found a direction. The official church did not satisfy the need. People tried Stormgade, where hundreds were frequently denied admission for lack of room. Or they tried the pastor in Lyngby, Bone Falch Rønne,[16] who in reality came to have as much historical significance as Mynster. Rønne cannot be compared to Mynster, either in stature or cultivation, but he had a lively sense for this subterranean unrest, both in the city and in the countryside. He founded the Lyngby Area Bible Society, an evangelical tract society, and in 1821 he founded The Danish Mission Society. Rønne was one of Lindberg's forerunners. He supported the participants in the religious awakening movement against government persecution, and he assembled a motley band of these restless souls around his pulpit, where no distinction was made between Moravian sympathizers, pietists, and orthodox Lutherans.

Mynster undoubtedly looked upon this unrest with displeasure. Rønne became a close friend of Lindberg, who often delivered vehement and provocative sermons in Rønne's church. In 1827 Lindberg concluded a sermon with these words: "So choose! No one can serve two masters! The way to Heaven, the way of faith, begins only in our earthly life. After death it is too late. . . . We live in evil times, when faith is mocked. Let us therefore separate ourselves from the world. Choose now! One cannot both follow Christ and the worldly wise."[17] On another occasion, he railed against false prophets: "They believed that God's blessing would reveal itself in wealth, but we know that the fate of the Church here in the world is opposition and the cross. Let us therefore be wary of these false prophets. Pastors, prophets, professors[18] use their offices as seductive sheep's clothing beneath which they conceal their false doctrines."[19]

Thirty years later we would hear exactly the same notes from Søren Kierkegaard, who had been only twelve years old at the time but who had grown up in a home in which the intellectual and spiritual climate had been defined by these awakenings. His father had had a connection with the Lyngby circle and had been a member of Rønne's Danish Mission Society, whose rural members had included Peter Larsen Skræppenborg, Christen Madsen, Rasmus Sørensen, Rasmus Ottesen, Kristian Kold, and Jens Jørgensen, all of whom began in the religious awakening movement and some of whom subsequently became founders of the peasant political movement.[20] As Lindberg did years later, Rønne undertook countless travels in rural areas, participating in religious assemblies and distributing his tracts, everywhere a helper and an awakener, the sworn ally of the common man in this difficult time of change and struggle. These were the times "when God's Word was costly, when afflictions were dire, and when the need was great,"[21] as Grundtvig later wrote to his daughter Meta, referring to the period when he published *The Church's Reply* (1825) in opposition to the quasi-rationalistic H. N. Clausen.[22]

Rønne was one of the few who supported Grundtvig unconditionally, calling him "the fiery interpreter of the truth." This said, however, it must be admitted that Rønne never became a prominent churchman and was only a footnote in church history. But an examination of Rønne's work in Lyngby and elsewhere throughout the country, his zeal, his naive faith in tracts, his deep understanding of the difficulties facing the common man — his focus on a faith that was just as easy and just as difficult for the simple people as for the learned — calls to mind Grundtvig's verse about Ansgar:[23]

> He was no mighty intellect,
> An evangelist in the field.
> Yet he was a tool in God's hand,
> Truly a Christian from the heart.[24]

While he was influenced by both the Stormgade meetinghouse and the Lyngby parsonage, M. P. Kierkegaard turned primarily to the former. He was, as mentioned, a member of a sort of governing board, the so-called

"Gehülfen," that stood behind the large Sunday meetings and took the initiative when the meeting room in Stormgade needed to be enlarged to accommodate six hundred people. Among this congregation were the majority of those who subsequently were associated with Grundtvig's vesper services at Frederik's Church and, later, with his congregation at Vartov. Had it not been for Mynster, the elder Kierkegaard would also have gone down the path to Grundtvig. The old man did not have an easy time of it in the mid-1820s. The peaceable years in Stormgade were over. The arrival of Grundtvig and Lindberg on the scene galvanized the religious awakenings. Mynster was sharply opposed to Lindberg in particular, who was on the frontline in the battle and who invited the hatred and disdain of the cultivated, particularly the clergy. The rebellion against the state church was underway.

Around 1830, when the Frederik's Church (then the German church, now Christian's Church) became available, an attempt was made to form a free congregation with Grundtvig as the central figure. Almost one hundred families signed a petition on behalf of establishing this congregation, but not the elder Kierkegaard. He sensed the beginning of a break with the state church, and his interest in the awakening movement did not extend that far. In a letter to the theologian Andreas Gottlob Rudelbach,[25] his sisters, who were ardent supporters of Lindberg, wrote,

> It has amazed me [*sic*] and a number of other people that old Kierkegaard has totally refused to lend public support to this congregation, claiming that he cannot or does not dare to do so, because he has two sons who are university students, who must obtain positions [in the state church]. Lindberg believes that the Kierkegaards are certainly not un-Christian people, but that they are among those who come to the Lord at night. He believes this also about young Kierkegaard [Peter Christian], particularly in view of the fact that he hasn't resumed his acquaintance with Grundtvig, . . . nor does he come to see Lindberg. . . . Lindberg now no longer believes that he [Peter Christian Kierkegaard] will do anything on behalf of Christianity before he has an official position, and he says, in jest, "if only he doesn't postpone it until he finds a better position."[26]

Here we have a portrait of the conscience-plagued, anxiety-ridden older brother, who often made things difficult for the two healthier and more decisive men in the family. Søren often used the word "pusillanimous" with respect to Peter Christian. Old Kierkegaard was certainly in agreement with Lindberg, but he found him too vehement and therefore would not support him. The Rudelbach sisters were deeply offended: "Among those who have any money, old Kierkegaard is the only one shabby enough to have responded that he will not give a shilling to Lindberg, because he does not approve of Lindberg's attacks upon individual persons."[27] Most of those who gave were very poor, "and these poor shoemakers and such really put rich Kierkegaard to shame."[28] Fear of Mynster probably played a role in his decision. Still, the elder Kierkegaard quietly followed along and was a subscriber to the *Theological Monthly,* to which Lindberg, Grundtvig, and the young Grundtvigians contributed.

When the movement for a free congregation appeared to falter, Lindberg began to hold religious assemblies at his home, "Lille Rolighed" [Little Serenity] out near a limekiln on the outskirts of Copenhagen. He was ready to break with the state church, and he became increasingly vehement in his anticlericalism. These religious meetings were the talk of the town in scandalized Copenhagen and even in the quiet Kierkegaard household. Naturally, the Rudelbach sisters were supporters of Lindberg. In a letter to her brother in which she describes a visit to the Kierkegaards, Juliane Rudelbach wrote:

> I really cannot understand young Kierkegaard [Peter Christian], and what is more, his parents cannot understand him. He seems to be burdened with both spiritual and physical weakness. . . . He was present at "[Little] Serenity," at the sermon by Lindberg that I mentioned. . . . In general, he seems to have no firmness or clarity whatever with respect to religious conflict and to the new church, but to waver this way and that, which, frankly speaking, I don't think is good.[29]

Here we have a picture of Peter Christian's irresolution while Lindberg was forcing people to make a choice and come to a decision.

Grundtvig, too, became uneasy and decided to hinder the formation of a free congregation and to spread oil on the waters troubled by Lindberg's meetings out at the limekiln, a move Søren almost certainly noticed. Here we have the root of the biased comparison of Lindberg and Grundtvig in the *Concluding Unscientific Postscript*. During this tempestuous time Søren also expressed concern about his brother's spiritual life:

> The truth is that Peter has never been young in the spiritual sense. He received a morbid impression of religion, and he has been so anxious and afraid of God that he has been lodged fast in pusillanimity — and God knows if he will become truly invigorated by daring to believe that God loves him. I have never been young in the physical sense, but spiritually I have always been a youth, and in a good sense. Overwhelmed by God, annihilated to less than a sparrow in his eyes, I have nonetheless been granted a certain courage and openness that has enabled me to engage myself with him in youthful fashion.[30]

Lindberg delivered the sermon mentioned above in the Rudelbach sisters' letter on December 26, 1831. Peter Christian was present, and eighteen-year-old Søren may have been there as well. According to the Rudelbach sisters, "The day after Christmas Lindberg preached on the text from the gospel, and since it is the only required text of the entire church year that deals with the martyrs, he seized the opportunity to preach an extraordinarily stern and blunt sermon in which he loudly and publicly proclaimed that at present there is not a single pastor in the entire *Danish* State Church, *not a single one*, who, like St. Stephen, would step forth and do battle for his Lord and Savior *now*, when it is most needed."[31]

Twenty-four years later Søren Kierkegaard would say exactly the same thing, addressing himself, as Lindberg had, to the common man against the deceptions with which the clergy had shrouded themselves. If Søren did not hear the sermon, it was certainly recounted to him at home by his terrified brother who, like Grundtvig and the younger Grundtvigians of the time, felt a certain reluctance and skepticism about the vehement Lindberg for stirring up unrest among the lower orders of society. In the early 1830s, Lindberg was one of the most ridiculed men in Copenhagen. All the newspapers published coarse rhymes or scurrilous articles about him. *The Copenhagen Post* wrote that he and his assembly, which was composed of the lowest, most uncultivated classes, were like "an old wound on a frail body, from which oozed so much poisonous and stinking venom that it infects the air,"[32] and noted that his religious assemblies were frequented by prostitutes.[33] Rarely before or since has a man been so publicly vilified with such malicious language.

Naturally, all the cultivated people remained silent, and Lindberg's few close friends were in doubt about what to do. "What makes me sad about the religious struggle," wrote one of the Rudelbach sisters, "is that now, with difficulties increasing every day, no one comes forth and offers to do battle at Lindberg's side, . . . and that *right now not one single pastor in all of Denmark is fighting for the cause of Christianity.* Lindberg stands alone now, but he is protected by Almighty God, who is certainly capable of leading him forth with a mighty arm, but who may perhaps allow him to become a martyr for his cause."[34] Lindberg had barely enough income to keep body and soul together, and for years he was forced to live on charity. University students often tried to create disturbances in order to disrupt his meetings, but one look at Lindberg (who was also enormous in stature) usually disabused them of that strategy. Lindberg himself remained calm and unruffled; he knew that he had cut to the quick.

In a regular column in *The Copenhagen Post,* entitled "Contributions to Knowledge about Magister Lindberg," Lindberg could read just how deeply he had cut.[35] He was even the target of slander from Germany, in a piece entitled "Ueber das Treiben der Zeloten in Kopenhagen," where he was labeled an underhanded, poisonous, evil-spirited deceiver, a seducer of the people, a disciple of Loyola, a fanatic, and a sophist.[36] On the streets there were demonstrations featuring pictures of Lindberg and the Devil; at the amusement park at Dyrehave, the Prince of Darkness was on display bearing the name "Magister Lindberg."[37] The jeers of the mob made it impossible for him to walk the streets in peace, and there were rumors that he was to be imprisoned and sent in exile to the remote island of Christiansø. Mynster wrote that scarcely "any of the enemies of Christianity have awakened so much offense as this Lindberg."[38]

It is no surprise that the elder Kierkegaard would not support Lindberg, and that Peter Christian shrank from doing so. As a twenty-year-old student, Søren experienced all this firsthand, though at that point he was probably unable to comprehend the full dimensions of the battle for the church. In all likelihood, he didn't understand that the dialectician Lindberg had pushed matters to such a point that from then on only a writer of scandalous journalism would really be able to awaken the common man and unmask the illusion collectively perpetrated by the clergy. More than twenty years later, Kierkegaard would find himself in exactly the same situation and would receive exactly the same treatment. But as a young man he could not have avoided seeing one thing clearly: that the principal issue for Lindberg had been the *common man,* which was why his father had followed Lindberg with conspiratorial interest. Lindberg was a man of the people, not because he had popular ideas and visions but because of his daily involvement with the common people in matters concerning their real problems and needs. He gave them advice and encouragement. They wrote to him from every part of the land, as is reflected by his enormous correspondence. At the same time, he was one of the most learned men in the country, famous all over Europe as a numismatist and specialist in Hebraic studies.

Søren Kierkegaard must have found this entire situation captivating, and he must have had it very much in mind when he wrote the *Concluding Unscientific Postscript* and *A Literary Review.* Here was a case of someone who "lived up to his character," who acted and related himself responsibly and directly to the ideas he espoused. This is where Kierkegaard reacted against Grundtvig, who was certainly in agreement with Lindberg but who helped moderate the situation and thus distanced himself from the common people who had trooped from Stormgade and Lyngby Church to gather around Lindberg. Perhaps this was the correct tactical move if Grundtvig wanted to promote peaceful growth. Grundtvig was a man of the times, but Lindberg was a man of the moment, a man of the street, and a man of rebellion. Gradually, Lindberg and the others participating in the awakening calmed down. But Grundtvig's evensong sermons at Frederik's Church never became what the meetings at the limekiln had been for the awakened of Copenhagen. The Rudelbach sisters were among those who felt abandoned by events and by the uncontroversial tone that Grundtvig had now adopted:

> Once again, it comes down to the fact that Grundtvig is just not suited to talk to simple people. They are unable to come to him in confidence or with an open heart. Of course, the reason for this is that Grundtvig has always maintained a limited network of acquaintances, which was what suited him, and has otherwise buried himself in his books and research. Now, when these ordinary people come to him, he treats them quite curtly and repels them, or is at any rate inaccessible to them. These poor people — who would stand their ground like lions in talking to unbelievers — when they stand before Grundtvig, whom they firmly believe to be an apostle, cannot say a word and therefore feel painfully rejected.[39]

The Rudelbach sisters almost certainly discussed this matter during their frequent visits to the Kierkegaard home, where passions were surely running high, especially when Lindberg and Frederik Hammerich also showed up. The elder Kierkegaard was torn, but he positioned himself most closely to Grundtvig, whose evensong services he attended when he didn't go to Stormgade, the meetinghouse of the Congregation of Brothers, where he could feel passionately and profoundly at home and removed from all the debate, where he had found comfort and edification in his youth.

But in addition to a father, there was also a mother in the Kierkegaard home on Nytorv. Kierkegaard researchers have expressed surprise that her son never mentions her. But the experts have not carefully considered Kierkegaard's categories of keeping silent and of speaking, where silence is precisely what determines the substance and richness of speech. This sort of silence is defined in opposition to the unending chatter "which taken in its entirety still does not constitute personal human speech of the sort that can be spoken by even the simplest person, who can only speak of a very few things, but who nonetheless does speak."[40] In my view, it is quite possible that Kierkegaard wrote the above-cited passage (from *A Literary Review*) with his mother in mind. But since he does not speak of her directly, it has been decreed (by those who do not properly understand Kierkegaard) that his mother was without significance and that his father's second marriage was a sort of misalliance, entered into hastily and under dubious circumstances. Thus, while the first wife was a Rachel, the second was only a Leah with whom the old man had to suffer for many years. And in Kierkegaard's journals some have found what they believed to be the son's views on the question of second marriages, as in a passage from 1839, where he reflected upon Genesis, the church, and marriage, citing a Greek passage by Athenagoras to the effect that second marriages are indecent and constitute a breach of marriage;[41] a passage from 1844, where a second marriage was described as only a mediocre reprint of the first;[42] and a passage from 1854, where Kierkegaard wrote of a weak sensualist, an old man who scarcely had the power of his senses left to him, who could not control his passions.[43] Scholars claim that Kierkegaard made these remarks with reference to his parents and to their marriage: his father was a sensual old man and his mother a seduced servant girl!

We do know something about Kierkegaard's relationship to his father, even if we don't have the whole story. We know that the son often complained about how severely his father had confronted him as a weak and sensitive boy with the demands of the ideal, which caused him a great deal of anguish. Nonetheless, in 1850 he wrote, "Then I came to terms with it religiously. Humanly speaking it has made me as unhappy as possible, but this pain was the basis on which I developed a brilliant intellectual life as an author. I came to terms with myself in this life. The anguish was frightful, but the satisfaction was all the greater. I can never thank God sufficiently for what has been given me."[44] This passage seems to sum up Kierkegaard's various statements about his relationship to his father.

But what about his silence with respect to his mother? In fact we do not know a great deal about her. Her name was Ane Sørensdatter Lund.[45] She was born in the parish of Brande in central Jutland. Like Michael Pedersen Kierkegaard's first wife, Kirstine Røyen,[46] she came from Jutland to Copenhagen as a servant girl, where she held a number of positions before entering Kierkegaard's service. When his first wife died in 1796, Ane Lund married him just over a year later. We know nothing about what sort of marriage it was, except that as the years passed and more children were born she became something of a center, or rather a point of equilibrium, in the often turbulent atmosphere of the Kierkegaard home, with its high-flying debates and the old man's melancholy — although Michael Pedersen was for the most part able to conceal that melancholy behind high spirits and irony (an art he managed to pass on to Søren, but not to Peter Christian). The mother could read, but probably could not write. We know that Peter Christian presented her with *Zion's Harp,* a hymnal that Lindberg had produced for his religious gatherings, and that she valued it highly. In her memoirs, Henriette Lund gave a couple of glimpses of her grandmother, based on remarks by others: "She was referred to in the family as a kind little woman with an unpretentious and cheerful turn of mind."[47] She couldn't keep up with the learned jargon of the three men in the family:

> She was therefore never more in her element than when a passing illness forced them ever so slightly back under her jurisdiction. . . . [S]he then wielded her scepter with delight, cosseted them, and protected them like a hen her chicks. Her motherly inclinations also agreed with the grandchildren in the family. Her plump little figure often had only to appear in the doorway of the nursery, and the cries and screams would give way to a hush.[48]

The picture isn't very revealing, but it nevertheless radiates coziness and maternal warmth.

In his memoirs, Hans Brøchner stated that his cousins viewed Søren Kierkegaard as "a frightfully spoiled and naughty boy who always hung on his mother's apron strings."[49] This accords with other things we know about little Søren, whose position as the youngest of seven children and whose fantasy-filled imagination and penchant for teasing had earned him a place as the family jester. Frederik Hammerich wrote, "He took us to his house one time, and there we saw his strangely gifted parents. The old Jutland hosier was a man who was always reading. He could work his way through philosophical systems, but nonetheless made the family's daily purchases at the market himself. I can still see him on his way home from the market, carrying a fat goose."[50] Eline Heramb,[51] who was Peter Christian Kierkegaard's sister-in-law, wrote,

> It was interesting . . . to hear the skill with which old Kierkegaard (who had originally been a wool dealer from Jutland and was now a well-to-do merchant) could join in the debate with his two gifted sons and always have a ready answer, even though the discussions concerned heaven and earth and everything imaginable in between. The old mother listened to this with admiration, but occasionally she would interrupt in order to calm things down when it seemed to her that they were getting too excited.[52]

These glimpses reveal all that we in fact know about Søren Kierkegaard's relationship with his mother. We have learned that as the youngest he hung on her apron strings. She was possessed of an uncomplicated warmth. With her, Søren could cry his heart out without inhibitions. He was reminded of this years after her death (she died in 1834, when he was twenty-one) when he was staying in Gilleleje,[53] where he had vacationed as a boy:

> I believe that I can see myself quite vividly as a little boy running about in my green jacket and gray trousers. But alas, I have grown older and cannot catch up with *myself.* Contemplating childhood is like contemplating a beautiful part of the country while riding backwards: one only becomes aware of the beauty of it at the moment, at the very instant, that it begins to disappear, and all I have left of that happy time is the ability to *cry like a child.*[54]

In his mother Kierkegaard encountered a simple person who was capable of silence and therefore also capable of speech, who was the source of many a proverb and many a serious comment that he never forgot. According to a detailed summary in the newspaper *The People's Friend,* in his eulogy of his brother Søren, Peter Christian said that "Søren Kierkegaard preserved many of his mother's words in his writings,"[55] which seems plausible in the light of the other information we have examined. In his autobiography, H. L. Martensen preserved another glimpse of Kierke-gaard's relation to his mother:

> My mother has told me that while I was abroad, he quite often came to her for news of me. In addition, she related something I will not leave out, that from time to time he stayed and sat with her awhile, and that she took great pleasure in his conversation. Once he came in deep sorrow and told her that his mother had died. My mother has repeatedly confirmed that never in her life (and she had had no little experience) had she seen a human being so deeply distressed as S. Kierkegaard was by the death of his mother. From this she felt she could conclude that he must have an unusually profound sensibility.[56]

But Kierkegaard shrouded his mother's memory in silence, and only his brother recognized which of the words in his writings stemmed from her. Nonetheless, in *For Self-Examination,* the last book he published prior to the long silence that preceded his attack on the church, we glimpse a portrait of her that is not quite as poetically retouched as the many portraits of his father. The first of the three discourses in this book is based on one of Kierkegaard's favorite texts, the first chapter of the epistle of James: "But become doers and not just hearers of the Word." Rarely was his style so popular and straightforward. One can even detect the Jutlandic speech of his childhood home: "Something wrong? Are you all right in the head?"[57] This latter sentence is very un-Copenhagen, but quite typical of West Jutland, and he must have heard his father or mother say it. In the passage in question he returned to the category of *silence,* which we recall from the sketch we have seen of the simple person in *A Literary Review.* Here we have a domestic portrait of the home on Nytorv, where the father was indeed the one who made the wheel turn, but the mother was the axle of stability:

> And you, O woman, indeed for you is reserved the ability to be the image of the Word's hearer and its reader, who does not forget. You comply fittingly with the Apostle's exhortation: a woman shall keep silent in the congregation; it is fitting. Neither does she occupy herself with preaching at home; it is unbecoming. No, let her be silent.

She treasures the Word in silence. Let her silence express the fact that she treasures the Word deeply. Don't you believe in silence? I do. . . . Let me describe for you such a woman, a hearer of the Word, who does not forget the Word. But do not be distracted by the description so that you yourself forget to become such a person! As stated, she does not speak in the congregation. She is silent. Neither does she talk about religion at home. She is silent. Nor is she like an absent-minded person, far away in distant regions. You sit and speak with her, and while you are sitting there you say to yourself, "She is silent. What does this silence mean?" She tends her house; she is very attentive, as though with her entire soul, even down to the most insignificant detail. She is joyful, sometimes full of jokes and merriment. She is the joy of the house, almost more so than the children. And just when you are sitting and looking at her you say to yourself, "She is silent. What does this silence mean?" And even if the person who is closest to her, to whom she is bound with indissoluble ties, whom she loves with all her soul, and who has a claim upon her confidence — if it could be imagined that he would say to her right out, "What does this silence mean? What are you thinking of? Because there is something behind all this, something you always seem to have in mind. Tell me what it is!" — she would not say it right out. At most she might say, evasively, "Are you coming to church with me on Sunday, then?" And then she speaks of other things. Or she says, "Promise to read a sermon aloud to me on Sunday!" And then she speaks of other things. What does this silence mean?

What does it mean? Yes, let us not search further for it. If she says nothing directly to her husband, we others cannot insist upon being told anything. No. Let us not search further for it, but let us consider that this silence is precisely what we need if the Word of God is to gain a bit of power over people.[58]

I have needed to give this sketch of Søren Kierkegaard's home and its climate in spite of the small number of sources that are available to us on the subject because this was the all-important background for his years as a university student in the 1830s, when, according to his journals, he pursued aesthetic interests as the poet he was. But he had a philosophical-dialectical talent that was dangerous to poetry. This dissonance was to cause him much anguish, as it also did with Heinrich Heine, whose path Kierkegaard paralleled quite closely for a time. Like Heine, Kierkegaard had a detective's eye for the disagreement between early and late Romanticism. Like Heine, Kierkegaard had the typical late Romantic taste for ironic playfulness, for humor, for concealment, for the interesting and the piquant — and as a counterpoint, a sense for folk songs and folk tales. He made plans for great aesthetic-philosophical works on Faust, Ahasuerus, and Don Juan. We hear a great deal about these plans. And during these years of ferment, like all young men, he enjoyed himself with his peers, in part as a protest against the atmosphere of his family home.

But despite a great deal of guesswork, we know very little else about his private life beyond the fact that the family (and particularly his anxiety-ridden brother) was worried about his attitude toward religion, and that his aesthetic paths might lead to perdition. Kierkegaard himself mentioned this subsequently. In 1838 his brother wrote in his diary, "[Søren] is now beginning to come closer not only to individual Christians (e.g., Lindberg) but also to Christianity."[59] In her memoirs, Lindberg's daughter Elise stated that at this time Søren Kierkegaard visited Lindberg every week together with a number of young Grundtvigians, the Fengers, the Hammerichs, and Peter Rørdam.[60] But at roughly the same time, Kierkegaard remarked to Vilhelm Birkedal that, "in the middle of all this nonsense about Christianity with which we are surrounded," he didn't think that the Grundtvigian view of the church was the key to the secret of Christianity.[61] The following lines from Kierkegaard's journals stem from the same period and reflect Lindberg's religious movement:

In general there are very few people who are capable of bearing the *Protestant* view of life. If it is truly to strengthen *the common man,* this [Protestant] view must either organize itself into small groups (separatism, conventicles, etc.) or approach Catholicism, in order in both cases to find a way of sharing life's burdens socially; this is something that only the most gifted individuals can do without. Christ indeed died for everyone, and also for me. But this "for me" must nonetheless be understood as meaning that he only died for me insofar as I belong to the many.[62]

This remark, which stands alone among all the aesthetic and philosophical reflections in the journal from 1838, was perhaps a contribution to the debates in the Kierkegaard home that were occasioned by Lindberg's campaign for the rights of the common man. I think I am correct in claiming that Lindberg's movement on the one hand and Kierkegaard's experience of his father on the other (both the son's view of his father's outward appearance as a sympathizer with unrest in the church and the son's more private experiences of his father, in the confidences his father shared with him) constitute the fundamental elements in Kierkegaard's youth, while all the aesthetic and philosophical elements are secondary materials that, as he explains in *The Point of View for My Activity as an Author,* were subsequently used in the service of "deception."

But we don't know much about Søren during these years. He was an observer. He associated with Lindbergians and Grundtvigians. He was one *among* them, not one *of* them. Even in his early youth he was incommensurable with the tendencies and opinions of his times. He was the individual who was looking for the single Archimedean point from which he could move the world. His father died and was then earnestly resurrected in the son's memory. Then Kierkegaard fulfilled his father's last wish by taking his theological examinations and thereafter made a pilgrimage to his father's peasant village in faraway western Jutland. Before his journey he wrote an entry in his journal in which he bade farewell to all the ecclesiastical unrest to which he had been witness in his youth:

> After abandoning every effort to find himself outside himself in existence, in relationships, or in his surroundings; when, after this shipwreck, the individual turns to what is highest; then, after this emptiness, the Absolute dawns for him, not only in its fullness but also in the responsibility he feels is his.[63]

This trip to Jutland was a journey both to the Continent in the external, geographical sense and to a continent within. The journals reflect dejection and elation, but are otherwise laconic. Their main feature is silence, especially after he arrived in Sædding. But occasional flashes betray profound reflections on two things that cast both shadow and light on this interior continent, this landscape that Kierkegaard sometimes believed to be barren heath:

> I am so listless and devoid of joy that I not only have nothing to fill my soul, but I cannot even conceive of anything that could possibly satisfy it — alas, not even the bliss of Heaven. To thee, O God, we turn for peace — but grant us also the blessed assurance that nothing can deprive us of this peace, *not we ourselves,* nor our foolish earthly wishes, nor my wild desires, nor my heart's restless craving![64]

Shadow and light: it is the memory of his father and the recollection of Regine back home in Copenhagen. He was accompanied on his pilgrimage by a sense both of joy and of perdition. He discerned within himself powerful forces that manifested themselves as both anxiety and courage: "My total mental and spiritual incapacity at present is frightful precisely because it is linked with a consuming longing, with a spiritual concupiscence — and yet it is so amorphous that I don't even know what it is I need."[65]

There he was, sitting in Ringkøbing, the last station on the way to Sædding, the place where it all began:

> I sit here entirely alone . . . counting the hours until I see Sædding. I cannot recall there ever having been any change in my father, and now I will see the places where as a poor boy he tended sheep, places for which I have felt homesickness because of his descriptions. What if I now were to fall ill and be buried in Sædding Cemetery! What a strange thought. His last wish for me is fulfilled. Could this really be the whole of my earthly destiny? In the name of God! Yet compared to what I owe him, the task was not so little. From him I learned what fatherly love is, and thus I received a notion of divine fatherly love, the only unshakable thing in life, the true Archimedean point.[66]

The next day he reached the little village on the heath and stayed with his father's sister. The journal says little, but in the few entries one hears the hidden currents of underground rivers. Here there was much to reflect upon: his father's confidences, the earthquake (concerning which he is also silent) — here, where his father, as a little shepherd boy numb with cold, had cursed God. The cemetery with the family graves, these strong wills, these fiery spirits, seared by passion, healed by faith. And what else? The mute saga of the common people of those days — now they were mould in the earth, shrouded in impenetrable silence. Was he the one through whom these strong spirits of the common people would find a voice? And the low, unsteepled church, where he himself had preached on the feeding of the people in the desert. "Let the dead bury their dead," he had said in his sermon. Christ "went among them as a shining example of how little a person needs; he who had no place to rest his head, his *bread* was to do his father's will."[67] "His father's will" was to be understood in two senses, and therefore this trip to the village of Kierkegaard's father's childhood was also to be a re-consecration.

He remained there for three days and then hurried home to the things he had longed for all during the journey: a young girl and the start of his work. He had come to equilibrium, and when he was in Aarhus waiting for the boat he wrote in his journal:

> Still, there is an equilibrium in the world. To one person God gave joys; to another he gave tears and permission to rest in his embrace every now and then. And yet the divine is reflected much more beautifully in the tear-dimmed eye, just as the rainbow is more beautiful than the clear blue sky.[68]

During these days in Aarhus, it was as though he felt crouched and ready to spring, as though he were borne by a wave. Right through the melancholy and tears he sensed a song, a recovery, powers being set free. Everything — the striking of the clock in the cathedral or the roll call of the soldiers across the street — was an omen of what lay ahead, shrouded in the fertile mystery of the future. He wrote a few more sentences while still in Jutland:

52

How glorious the sound of the dragoons blowing the call to assembly. It is as if I already heard the hoofbeats as they charged. Listen, they are victorious, the cry of victory resounds in the air! And yet, what are all other calls compared to the one the archangel will someday blow, shouting, "Awake, you who are asleep, the Lord is coming!"[69]

CHAPTER FIVE

The Coteries of the Cultivated

The previous chapter described Søren Kierkegaard's home during the 1830s, when Kierkegaard was a young university student and a first-hand spectator of the vehement ecclesiastical struggles that had as their central figure Jacob Christian Lindberg, the campaigner for those who took part in the revivals and opponent of the state church. In those days the church and the upper class were bound together in a humanistic-religious elite culture. If anyone launched an attack against religion, as Lindberg did, the humanistic side also felt itself under attack, and vice versa. Jakob Peter Mynster and his successor Hans Lassen Martensen (who attempted to provide a more detailed justification for the synthesis) were among the most prominent representatives of this elite world. What was to be believed and taught throughout the country was defined from the pulpit and the episcopal chair with such authority and emphasis that all discussion was cut off, at least so far as the lower classes were concerned. The religious awakening movements were viewed as forms of rebellion and subversion to be punished with fines and imprisonment, at least when ordinary people like Christen Madsen or Peter Larsen Skræppenborg were involved.

The situation was more difficult with Lindberg. He had had the benefit of a first-rate university education, with access to the whole of the elite culture. Lindberg was always the superior dialectician in debate and had in fact forced his rationalistic opponents to moderate their views and beat a cautious retreat from their positions, which is why he was regarded with such inconceivable hatred. The hatred was all the more inconceivable because Mynster, in his heart of hearts, was privately in agreement with him: "It is a shame that we, who are in agreement with Lindberg with respect to the substance of the matter, are unable to extend a fraternal hand to him because of the manner in which he fights for the truth," he said to Rasmus Møller in 1832.[1] So, it was the *manner* of Lindberg's campaign — the awakening, the involvement of the common man. Perhaps there was a hidden social fear involved. The manner, not the message, was the reason Mynster and the others remained silent and allowed the mob to abuse Lindberg. Something similar would underlie the attitude toward Kierkegaard's battle with *The Corsair* and his campaign in *The Moment*. Kierkegaard did not understand these dynamics in the 1830s, and even afterwards he probably did not understand that his campaign against the amalgamation of religion and humanism in the Mynster-Martensen view of Christianity could also have social consequences. But the common people understood it very well. They understood that Kierkegaard's campaign was also an attack on the social-political-religious synthesis that constituted the "establishment," the privileged elite culture that naturally depended upon social arrangements. Kierkegaard summarized this entire synthesis under the term "cultivation" or "culture" [*Dannelse*].

By virtue of his upbringing, of the polish Kierkegaard received from aesthetic circles and from his wide-ranging aesthetic studies during his early years; by virtue of his remarkable intellectual abilities and his university studies, culminating in the doctoral degree: by virtue of all this, Kierkegaard more than anyone had both the form and the content of culture. He was a natural adherent of the triumvirate that determined taste, faith, and knowledge in Denmark: *the University* (Johan Nicolai Madvig[2] and Martensen), *the Church of Our Lady* (Mynster), and *the Royal Theatre* (Johan Ludvig Heiberg and especially his wife, Johanne Luise).[3] Kierkegaard admired this aristocracy of intellect all his life, even when he was attacking it, and unlike his awkward brother, he got on very well with it. He could manage the tenor of the times as few others could. The spirit of the age ran the gamut from wit to sentimentality, and despite a crepuscular sadness, it was salted with irony. As has been mentioned, Kierkegaard cultivated Heinrich Heine. The tenor of the times was one in which dialectics became a cloak for a certain coyness as well as for deeper feelings that were often consumed by the dialectical play itself, play that transformed all impulsiveness into a reciprocal wariness that pulled everyone down to the same level — a cautiousness that could also be called tact. The tenor of the times was a sociable tone of animated conversation that dulled the edge of all originality and harbored a skepticism directed against everything original, particularly when it was encountered in the simpler classes, whether on city streets or in the wooden clogs of rural life. Hans Christian Andersen was to feel this until he, too, learned the tone, the sarcasm, the hidden irony he incorporated in his exquisitely polished miniatures of world-class art, his fairy tales, or better, his tales. But all this meant that the times were lacking in pathos and passion.

At first, Kierkegaard felt quite at home in a culture in which Mynster represented religion, Madvig scholarly knowledge, and Heiberg aesthetics. And they long viewed him as one of their own. Naturally there was something a bit clumsy about his first works; people could scarcely understand his intention, but they read him with admiration for his lively, subversive style, for the interesting, the piquant, the demonic element, for his irony and humor. Kierkegaard's early works were read as we could never read them, on the basis of certain features in their design that were the common property of the times, features that were conducive to what might be called conspiratorial participation in the prevailing cultural climate. The style of his early works captured the tenor of the times better than those of any other writers, so that even though these works naturally left a rather disturbing aftertaste (as Kierkegaard intended), no one noticed that the melody was not that of the times. In his refined and underhanded way, Kierkegaard had a definite intention behind the aesthetic disguise of his indirect communication. He had constructed his books as bombs that would explode well after they had hit their mark. To further the confusion, simultaneously with the publication of *Either/Or* Kierkegaard published *Two Edifying Discourses,* dedicated to his father, "former hosier here in the city." We recall how surprised Mynster was at that dedication.

Johanne Luise Heiberg, the muse of the period, exemplified the style of the times; she was compelled to be an even better actress in the parlor than on the stage. She was a child of the common people, and the fundamental elements in her genius were passion and spontaneity. With her superior intelligence, she became the mistress of her own origins and gifts and transformed them into the dazzling flirtatiousness of a many-faceted persona, movingly intimate and even engagingly provocative, though of course not unseemly. She was the rage of the era of the vaudeville, a theatrical form that was foreign to her true nature. Her greatest vaudeville triumphs involved a bit of song and some intrigue, as when she played the female character in stage couples such as Hans and Trine or Jochum and Lisbeth.[4] All this was alien to her real talent, which lay in pathos and passion. When finally she was to play Lady Macbeth, the very role for her, she was so corseted in the style of the times — replete with leveling envy, subtle nuances, and innuendo — that she couldn't do it. But when as a mature woman she again took up the part of Juliet, the role of her youth, Kierkegaard, with the seismographic sensitivity that made him a genuine critic, took careful note both of the difficulty facing Heiberg and of the special character of her talent. Kierkegaard's particular preoccupation was with the question of repetition, but as a true critic he illustrated the issue by embodying it in her.

In the middle of the religious period of his writings (when people in the worldly and sophisticated cultural circles of Copenhagen were asking whether he had now become pious, publishing collections of sermons) Kierkegaard published *The Crisis and a Crisis in the Life of an Actress,* analyzing the relationship between perfectibility and an actress's metamorphosis. It is a very enigmatic and brilliant essay, one that surely touched Johanne Luise Heiberg's vital center (but most of all touched Kierkegaard's own). It is closely related to *The Point of View for My Activity as an Author,* which stems from the same period. It shows a new interpretation of the concept of repetition and presents the notion of stage fright that is transformed into composure and ease onstage. Even Martensen puts in an appearance here as the senior court preacher who preaches only infrequently, so that when he does preach, the difficulties become quite perilous. And if one has put one's life at stake, the difficulties become even greater, "because not only with respect to the truth, but also with respect to curiosity, 'the blood of martyrs is the seed of the Church'."[5] And against this background Kierkegaard mounts a self-defense:

Nonetheless, the completely unselfish servants of the truth have always had the custom of associating very freely with the people. They have never played hide-and-seek with the crowd so that they could then play the game of surprise on the rare occasions when they present themselves as objects of astonishment. On the contrary, they have always shown themselves in their everyday attire, have lived with the common man, have conversed in the streets and alleys, renouncing every claim to respect.[6]

In reality the whole piece is a self-examination and a self-defense disguised as an aesthetic-dramaturgic analysis, all of which served Kierkegaard well at the time. He was writing *The Point of View for My Activity as an Author,* a work that was something of an *ex poste* rationalization, so that once again an aesthetic work would be followed by a religious one, just as had been the case years earlier with *Either/Or.* But those who read Kierkegaard's discussion of this work in his papers, where he keeps returning to this little piece in order to make it fit dialectically into the system of his life and writings, will find the aesthetics a bit weak. It is this little work on the theatre he has in mind when he reflects upon unrest, playfulness, coquetry, and, especially, *reliability.* Reliability is the existential touchstone that makes it possible to defend all the playfulness, secretiveness, and style:

When taken in the sense of finitude's hubbub, unrest is something one soon tires of. But unrest in the significant sense, the unrest of infinity, a joyous and lively originality that stirs the waters in a rejuvenating, refreshing, and healing fashion — this is a great rarity. And it is in this sense that she is unrest. Yet this unrest signifies something more, and something very great. It signifies the first fieriness of essential genius. . . . It reveals something elementally inexhaustible, like the wind or the sounds of nature. It reveals that her playfulness has an inexhaustible wealth, which again and again simply makes clear that she possesses much more. It reveals that her coquetry . . . is nothing other than a happy, innocent spirit in its joyous, triumphant awareness of its own indescribable good fortune. It is therefore not

59

really coquetry, but is yet another incitement to the spectator, and in fact assures him of the reliability of the entire performance, providing an absolute guarantee of the exuberance [that is, vouching absolutely for the integrity of the actress's animated performance].[7]

In the external form of his aesthetic works Kierkegaard could well call to mind one of Heiberg's performances on the stage — the ability to be simultaneously deceptive and truthful, the playing with thematic nuances, the coquettish crackle of the style — but under it all there was a reliability and a place of calm in the midst of agitation. Here, as in most places, this inner agitation was not a psychological category but a sense of depth, an existential commitment that undergirded her posture and thus guaranteed the reliability and honesty of the performance. At bottom Kierkegaard's essay was also an attack on the public, which admired without understanding. Thus Heiberg's joy did not consist in the joy she produced for others, but in the possibility of metamorphosis she possessed in herself, which in turn was a product of the passage of time — and of her own spirit's conquest of time.

And, finally, Johanne Luise Heiberg possessed what was lacking in the cultivated coterie to which she belonged and was particularly lacking in her husband, Johan Ludvig Heiberg: a fresh and lively originality, an elemental inexhaustibility, a passion that was broken into many facets and generated a smoldering intensity precisely because it was prevented from bursting into flame. Kierkegaard himself had firsthand knowledge of this sort of torment, which was precisely what was painful in the times. But by 1848, Kierkegaard had become older, and what once had been present became recollection. He, too, had once been young and fiery, had ridden daringly upon ideas, had vaulted over the stars and down into the abyss. His contemporaries had admired him and the envious had carped. And with a half-concealed echo of self-recognition, he now wrote,

Time has asserted its rights. Some things have been consigned to the past. But now the ideality of recollection will cast a brilliant light upon the entire performance, an incarnation that was not present even in those first days of youth. Only in recollection is there absolute rest, and this is precisely why there is also the quiet fire, the imperishable glow of the eternal. And she rests reassured in the eternity of her essential genius. She has no childish or wistful longing after the flames of what has disappeared. Her metamorphosis has left her too ardent and too rich for that. Like an idealizing light, this pure, reassuring, and rejuvenating recollection will illuminate the entire performance, which will become completely transparent in that illumination.[8]

He knew that she was possibly the only person who would understand him on the metamorphosis that reveals the idea, the notion of reliability, the repetition of the role that makes it imperishable in the glow of the genius of recollection. (During this period he needed someone with whom he could share his ideas, and he established a connection with another child of the common people, Rasmus Nielsen.[9] Nielsen took hold of everything, but understood little.) This little essay on Johanne Luise Heiberg as an actress, which is of such decisive significance for the understanding of Kierkegaard, is also one of the final steps in his long battle against the coteries of the cultivated. Kierkegaard's relations with those coteries had been strained both by the overall design of his undertaking on behalf of the religious ideal and by his personal background in the family home on Nytorv.

He had given an account of his relation (or misrelation) to his times in *A Literary Review,* which had analyzed Mrs. Gyllembourg's[10] tale *Two Ages.* *A Literary Review* was another doubly reflective work in which Kierkegaard searchingly investigated both the spirit of the times and his own spirit, combining the two to create the basis for a joint assault directed both against his times and against that portion of himself that shared the spirit of the times. He juxtaposed the revolutionary age with his own present age, which had been undermined by reflection:

> The age of revolution is essentially passionate. Therefore it is essentially *cultivated.* The elasticity of the inner being is indeed the measure of essential cultivation. A serving girl who is essentially in love is essentially cultivated. A man of the common people who has an essential and passionate commitment to an important decision is es-

sentially cultivated. A superficial and fragmentary set of manners based upon an inner emptiness, the colorful display of swaggering weeds in comparison to the humble bowing of the blessed grain, . . . is mere form and affectation.[11]

And further:

> The revolutionary age is essentially passionate. Therefore it has *not abolished the principle of contradiction.* It can become either good or evil, and whichever way it chooses, the impetus of passion is such that it must be recognizable, that the traces left by an action must mark its progress or its perdition. A decision must be reached. And this again is redemptive, because "decision" is the magic little word for which existence has respect. On the other hand, if the individual refuses to act, then existence cannot help. . . . Therefore one cannot simply accuse a highly reflective age of lacking strength, for it may have a great deal of strength that is being wasted in the sterility of reflection.[12]

With this comment Kierkegaard turned his guns on his own times. In sum:

> The present age is essentially *reasonable, reflective, without passion, flaring up in fickle enthusiasm and shrewdly relaxing in indolence.* . . . If one can say that the age of revolution *goes astray* [*farer vild*], one can say that the present age *goes badly* [*farer ilde*].[13]

Kierkegaard believed that his age could not make a revolution:

> A revolutionary but passionless and reflective [age] transforms the expression of strength into *a dialectical tour de force: it permits everything to continue to exist but cunningly deprives it of meaning. Instead of culminating in a rebellion, it ends by exhausting the inner reality of things in a reflective tension that permits everything to continue to exist while transforming the whole of existence into something ambiguous.* . . . The springs of life's relationships — which are only themselves when they have the passion to differentiate qualitatively — lose their elasticity.[14]

Both between the lines and in the lines themselves, the book is an attack on Kierkegaard's own principal tendency, reflection and dialectics. In place of these he proposed coming to a halt, deciding, acting (the leap, if you will) by means of which reflection, which in other respects and in itself is something negative, becomes a tool to be used, and thus something positive. The tool of reflection is to be put to use on the one hand exposing religious illusions (and the cultural illusions with which religious illusions are connected), and on the other hand to direct attention to the immediate, to the simple — indeed, to the common man. And this meant directing attention to the common man not as a political entity or object but as the individual whose pathos remains grounded in the principle of contradiction or (to use the decisive category that was truly impressed upon Kierkegaard by his father and by the Copenhagen religious awakenings) the standard of good and evil, right and wrong, honesty and dishonesty. These are disjunctions of which the common man had an unshakable and instinctive grasp, quite apart from any reflection or knowledge. Kierkegaard expressed this succinctly: "Reflection is a snare in which one is caught, but with the inspired leap of religion the situation is transformed: it becomes the catapult that casts one into the embrace of the Eternal."[15] Kierkegaard's own situation could not be stated more concisely than this, because he knew that

> reflection is and remains the most tenacious creditor in existence. Up to now, reflection has quietly bought up options on all the possible outlooks on life, but it cannot purchase the eternal life-view of the essentially religious. On the other hand, by means of spectacular deceptions reflection can lure people away from all else, and by reminding people of the past it can discourage them from all else.[16]

Here we find a statement that points far into the future, because this little work also contains the presuppositions that will undergird Kierkegaard's attack on the church, an attack that was a necessary consequence of his position and his intentions: "They want to permit the entire Christian terminology to continue to exist while knowing covertly that nothing decisive is supposed to be meant by it."[17] But Kierkegaard had indeed noted where the ambiguity and the aestheticism of the cultivated classes was leading:

> The tension of reflection finally establishes itself as a principle. And just as *enthusiasm is the unifying principle* in a passionate age, so *envy* becomes the *negatively unifying principle* in a passionless and highly reflective age. . . . Close air always becomes noxious; thus, when it is not ventilated with action, with events, closed-in reflection becomes the most reprehensible envy.[18]

These words were written with a personal emphasis: not only in his own day, but all the way up to our times, Kierkegaard has been persecuted by the concealed envy of his inferiors, as I have examined elsewhere.[19]

And finally, the age of reflection created that irresponsible abstraction, "the public," which was at the mercy of the press's power of suggestion:

> The public is not a people, not a generation, not a group of contemporaries, not a congregation, not an association, none of these particular groups of human beings, because all of these are only what they are by virtue of some concretion. Indeed, not a single member of the public has any essential engagement. . . . The public is everything and nothing; it is the most dangerous of powers and the most insignificant. One can address an entire nation in the name of the public, and yet the public is less than one single actual person, however unimportant that person may be.[20]

The public was precisely what resulted when the age of reflection abolished the principle of contradiction: "The existential expression of abolishing the principle of contradiction is to be in contradiction with oneself,"[21] Kierkegaard stresses yet again. Therefore the public exists in a state of "chatter," which is "the abolition of the passionate distinction between remaining silent and speaking. Only the person who is essentially capable of remaining silent is capable of speaking essentially; only the person who is essentially capable of remaining silent is capable of acting essentially."[22] To return to a passage cited in the previous chapter, "Taken in its entirety, all this talk still does not constitute personal human speech of the sort that can be spoken by even the simplest person, who can only speak of a very few things, but who nonetheless does speak."[23]

But how was Kierkegaard to battle against such times? Kierkegaard was engaged in an inner conflict with himself, a self he recognized as an expression of the very age he described, of whose poisonous qualities he was all the more aware. He concluded his book with several pages which seem rather offhand but which are of decisive significance for our understanding of him. Here he wrote that the person who is a child of the times but who wishes to fight against those times cannot do so with *authority*, as someone recognizable, as a prophet who wishes to lead a lost generation back to time-honored ways of doing things. Nowadays, the leaders of the opposition must "be without authority, precisely because they have come to a divine understanding of the diabolical principle of leveling; they will be *unrecognizable*, like plainclothes police, and will keep their various distinctions concealed, giving support only negatively, by repulsion."[24]

Only by means of an action that involves *suffering* would the unrecognizable one dare to help leveling in its progress, and by means of this same suffering action he will pass judgment on the instrument used. He does not dare defeat leveling straightforwardly. That would be the end of him, because it would be acting with authority. But in his suffering he will defeat it and will thereby express once again the law of his existence, which is not to command, govern, or lead, but to serve while suffering, to help indirectly.[25]

This lengthy section does not display dialectical clarity, but it reveals one of the basic intellectual presuppositions underlying Kierkegaard's indirect method of approaching his age. From a Christian point of view Kierkegaard found it important not to revert to the orthodox doctrinal or old-fashioned Lutheran structures but — precisely because he was a child of the age of reflection — to bring Christianity into reflection, thereby basing it upon the existential, upon the individual in a situation of choice and decision. This would simultaneously save the established order but destroy its vision, which was the synthesis of culture and Christianity (i.e.,

Mynster and Martensen). Here we have the origin of the slogan that Kierkegaard later employed repeatedly: *"Without authority, to make people aware."* This is the basis of that great arsenal he titled *Concluding Unscientific Postscript.*

Thus *A Literary Review* was a sketch of Kierkegaard's cultivated age, the time of reflection and leveling, and was also a description of the position from which one could launch an attack on that age — if one had the disease of the age in one's own blood. Using the category of the individual, which is based on the principle of contradiction, this position formed a dialectical counterpoint that was in striking opposition to the age. Another counterpoint could be found in the situation of the common man, the simple people who found themselves outside of (or subordinate to) the exclusive circles or coteries that set the cultural tone of the times. This is what led Kierkegaard to his reflections about the wise man and the simple man in the *Concluding Unscientific Postscript,* and it is this that formed the background for the particular tactics he chose for his indirect attack on cultivation. In 1848 he discussed this point quite openly in his journals:

> Melancholic as I was, and with my understanding of the Christian notion of human equality, I have lived year after year in such a manner that, at first, all the important people were critical of me. And I was well aware of this. Later on they concluded that my way of living was treason against them, because I ought to have become a member of their synagogue. And finally they became accustomed to it. This was how I lived, willing to talk to and associate with everyone on the street, completely oblivious to every form of respectability. And then what? Then I was attacked, and by whom? By the important people? Alas, no — that would have made sense. No, I was attacked by the crazy tribunes of the people (who are just the sort of people needed in order to produce this confusion) who are fighting for equality! And I am attacked for pride and exclusiveness! . . . The way the world is nowadays, pride and exclusiveness consist solely in avoiding the mass of people, in never being seen on the street, etc. . . .
>
> Alas, this is the difference between blind passion and honest zeal. I have seen very clearly what all the coteries are, especially the aristo-

cratic coterie. I have always expressed both joy and enthusiasm for the excellent properties they possess. And, showing all due respect, I have taken careful aim at the untruth in the coterie, at the deception, etc. My tactic has always been to sow discord in the coteries. . . . The great coterie is Mynster, Heiberg, Martensen, and company, because Mynster was a part of it, even if he never condescended to participate straightforwardly. This coterie thus intended to destroy me by means of negative resistance. Then there was the fortunate circumstance that I venerated Mynster so absolutely. This was an annoyance to them, and in fact the coterie could not get the rumor mill running. Then time passed and Heiberg became less and less active. Furthermore, he saw that he had been wrong, that I had absolutely no intention of becoming an aesthetician. Perhaps he even had a bit of a feeling of having wronged me. (It was in fact Heiberg whom I had originally targeted in order to break up the aesthetic coterie.) The coterie is weak. So I took his mother and celebrated her. . . . And now his wife — and for safety's sake a little wizardry against Martensen, in order that the coterie not be too pleased with all this. . . .

I am fighting for the individual, and it is true that the Kingdom of Denmark has been and remains the most barren ground for this, because here everything is coteries. But wherever there is a coterie, I am careful to choose one member, whom I venerate or draw close to me precisely in order to weaken the coterie. The most amusing case is that of Grundtvig. He has been attacked, among other reasons, because of his party. And nonetheless I have been successful in maintaining a sort of high-spirited relationship with him, which very much embitters his party.[26]

"It is true that I was born for intrigue," Kierkegaard wrote. Alas, yes. The memoirs and correspondence of his contemporaries make sad reading: they had absolutely no inkling of his cleverly mounted campaign. He might as well have stayed home and played with tin soldiers. None of the coteries mentioned him in these years around 1848 or in the 1840s generally, when his great works appeared. Not one word in Grundtvig's letters, or in Mynster's, Madvig's, or H. N. Clausen's memoirs of the period. Nor in Martensen's memoirs, which make mention of Martensen's encounter with Kierkegaard as a young man and, of course, of the year 1855, is there one word about the years in between. Nor in the case of Johanne Luise Heiberg, whose memoirs depict these years in great detail, is there one word (despite the fact that such books as *Either/Or, Repetition,* and probably *Prefaces* lay in her husband's study), excepting, of course, mention of Kierkegaard's articles on her reprise of the role of Juliet. We do not hear a single word concerning Kierkegaard's book about Johanne Luise Heiberg's mother-in-law.

Kierkegaard was certainly admired. He had a reputation for brilliance, and as the son of a wealthy hosier he could afford to write weighty tomes. But the better sort of people, the Mynster-Heiberg-Madvig coterie, nonetheless kept him at arm's length or ignored him. After all, he was nobody. He lacked the support that comes with an official position, and he never received a titular appointment such as professor or councillor of state. Councillor Kierkegaard — impossible, laughable! Furthermore, he was a comic figure of the streets that conversed with anyone and everyone — experimenting, people said. Martensen, at any rate, avoided him when he saw him on the horizon. Mynster shook his head. He was clever enough to realize that Kierkegaard's devotion to him was not what it appeared to be. Finally, thank God, came the attack by *The Corsair* — it would do him some good. In her memoirs Johanne Luise Heiberg has a chapter entitled *"The Corsair,"* noting that

> scandal at the expense of one's neighbor was the order of the day. This new fashion of attacking private individuals attracted much attention and secured a great circulation for the journal. Everyone who was not the object of its attacks found it "enormously amusing" until they themselves were attacked. Then they found it scandalous and infamous.[27]

But not one word about Kierkegaard — the conspiratorial admirer of Johanne Luise Heiberg herself and of her mother-in-law — Kierkegaard, who had regularly been a target of caricature and mockery in *The Corsair* during this period.

The entire campaign of intrigue that Kierkegaard wrote of was an illusion. On the basis of his great works he believed that he was significant, that he had something to say, that he alone was capable of lodging a protest against the abuses of *The Corsair* — not to mention capable of reintroducing Christianity into polite society, where the theatre went to church and the church went to the theatre and everyone was a Christian. Even Madvig sat devoutly in the Church of Our Lady. And even Heiberg gave his Hegelianism a religious gloss and remarked to his personal chaplain Martensen: "It has come to this: nowadays individuals will only obey the most supreme and immovable authority, the absolute, God. All intermediate authorities (earthly, human authorities) have lost their power and respect."[28] This of course could easily bring to mind Kierkegaard, who certainly would have replied, Yes, God is a theatre director who cannot be fired! Heiberg expressed his view of life concisely in a letter to his wife: "The true art of living is to enjoy the good wherever one encounters it, without being disturbed in the enjoyment by the shortcomings that are found in everything." This was exactly Kierkegaard's view of Heiberg. But however all that may be, if one sifts through the period's memoirs and correspondence for a reflection of Kierkegaard and his works during the 1840s, one finds almost nothing: silence or hostility and misunderstandings such as those in Birkedal and Martensen.

Kierkegaard could be admired, of course, but no account was taken of him. He was and remained incommensurate with his times, and it is also in this sense of the term that he was extraordinary. This gradually became clear to Kierkegaard himself, which is why the final volume of his papers contains so many pieces "About Myself." Nor was any impression made in these circles by his campaign in *The Moment* or by his death. Such an outbreak of madness was the sort of thing one could expect from an eccentric like Kierkegaard. Johanne Luise Heiberg did not waste a single word on *The Moment,* but was consumed with her struggle with Frederik Høedt and with his and Michael Wiehe's exodus to the Court Theatre.[29] Not one of them was present at Kierkegaard's burial. Martensen thought it scandalous to bury him after a funeral in the nation's principal church and on a Sunday. He had made his own coffin and now he had to lie in it. Only Copenhagen's poor accompanied him to his grave.

CHAPTER SIX

The Wise and the Simple

Kierkegaard made little tactical maneuvers to break up the coteries of the cultivated, who politely ignored or avoided him. His pseudonymous works had placed a torpedo under the ark, but by 1846 he had not yet reached the point at which his project was completed and he could retreat quietly. So in *Concluding Unscientific Postscript*, he focused upon the complex of problems that concerned him. The book was both an explanation of his pseudonymous campaign and an attempt to strike a blow at the Denmark of Johan Ludvig Heiberg and H. L. Martensen, where a religiously disguised Hegelianism was enjoying an Indian summer. Kierkegaard considered the attack necessary since, despite Jakob Peter Mynster, the culture of the "age of cultivation" was caught in an internal self-contradiction, because (as Kierkegaard repeatedly stated) it had abolished the principle of contradiction. Therefore the culture lacked passion, and its ideas evolved into mere principles. The many who applauded Johanne Luise Heiberg became nothing but an enthusiastic public and had betrayed the simple man's understanding that, after all, there must be a difference between good and evil, right and wrong, honesty and dishonesty. Of course, everybody believed in this dichotomy (everybody was a Christian, after all) but it had been curiously blurred by the climate that emanated from pulpit and theatre.

It was thus against this background that Kierkegaard inserted into the *Postscript* a passage in which he discussed the problem of simplicity, paralleling his discussion in *A Literary Review*. Throughout the latter work he had disguised himself as "the unrecognizable one"; in the *Postscript* he appeared as "the simple wise person." Here he introduced the category of "the differences," that is, the differences between the cultivated and gifted, on the one hand, and the simple and untutored, on the other.

He spoke of the difficulty of becoming subjective. Naturally, everyone was of course a subject, but it was precisely here that the difficulty lay,

> because every person has a strong natural desire and tendency to become something other and more than a subject. This is how it is with all apparently insignificant tasks: their apparent insignificance is precisely what makes them infinitely difficult, because the task does not lend support by sounding a direct summons to action. On the contrary, the task works against him, so that infinite efforts are required merely to discover the task: that is, to discover that *this* is the task. . . . To consider the simple things, to consider what the simple person knows, is extremely forbidding, because even with the utmost effort the difference does not become at all obvious to the sensate person. No, then what is grandiose is splendid in a quite different fashion.[1]

With these words Kierkegaard set out upon the path of a series of reflections that continue throughout the entire length of this large book, reflections on topics including not only the concepts of objectivity and subjectivity, but also those of paradox and existence. Throughout all of his extensive analyses, these concepts maintain their tangible incarnation in the simple person or the common man. In the lengthy passage that follows, we see a reflection of the way in which Kierkegaard put this idea into practice in the streets and alleys. The background for this passage is a consideration of the category of the "world-historical," a category with which N. F. S. Grundtvig, among others, was so engaged:

> In the world-historical process, God is metaphysically laced into a half-metaphysical, half-aesthetic/dramatic corset of convention, which is immanence. This produces a devil of a God. . . . First, then, the ethical (becoming subjective) and thereafter the world-historical. In his heart of hearts, surely even the most objective person is in fun-

damental agreement with what has been set forth here, namely that the wise person ought first understand the same thing that the simple person understands and ought to feel himself obligated by the same thing that obligates the simple person — and that only after this ought he proceed to the world-historical. First, then, the simple. But naturally this is easy for the wise person to understand, or why else do we call him wise? The understanding of this takes only an instant, and at that very instant he comes into full swing with the world-historical. The same undoubtedly holds for him with respect to my simple remarks: he has understood them instantaneously, and in the same instant he has gone much further. If only I could engage a wise person in conversation for a moment longer, because I would be happy to be the simple person who stops him with the following simple observation: *isn't simplicity exactly what the wise person finds most difficult to understand?* . . . Is it an insult to the wise person to focus attention upon him like this, so that the simplest becomes the most difficult merely because he is the one who must deal with it? Absolutely not. . . . When the child chatters away, his chatter is perhaps simple enough, and when the wise person says exactly the same thing, it has perhaps become the most ingenious of things. This is how the wise person relates himself to simplicity. When he enthusiastically venerates it as the highest, it honors him in turn, because it is as if, in him, the simple became something else, even though it in fact remains the same. The more the wise person considers simplicity, then, . . . the more difficult it becomes for him. And yet he feels himself seized by a profound humanity that reconciles him with the whole of life, namely that the difference between the wise person and the simplest person is merely this vanishingly small difference: that *the simple person knows the essential thing* that the wise person little by little *comes to know* that he knows or *comes to know* that he does not know — but what they know is the same.[2]

Here we have a key intersection in Kierkegaard's philosophy of existence, where philosophy with its web of conceptual definitions encounters the simple, which makes the same points that philosophy makes, but does so in immediacy. Thus speculation is prevented from lapsing into proud self-sufficiency because it is bound fast by the profound humanity that understands humanness [*Menneskelighed*] as human equality [*Menneske-Lighed*].

This was not only a warning and a challenge to the culture of "cultivation"; it was also an indication of what was being held in reserve in case the cultivated ignored the challenge, namely the common man, the hope of the future. In that case, the established order would have forfeited its rights, and the time of revolution would be at hand. In that case, the state church would be an illusion, and state and church would have to be separated. Kierkegaard was here laying the groundwork for the attack on the church that came a decade later. But (and this is one reason for the length of the *Postscript*) the difficulty in this case was that, unlike Jacob Christian Lindberg or Girolamo Savonarola, Kierkegaard could not step forward with authority and chastise his times. He was himself a part of that which had to be chastised. The products of Kierkegaard's own soul-searching, these books were also a stage in his own self-education: he himself was their reader just as the others were. He was a poet, one of the people to whom life's "differences" were important, and thus he had to express himself indirectly:

> The pathos does not consist in testifying to eternal happiness, but in transforming one's own existence into a testimony to it. The poetic pathos is a pathos of difference, but existential pathos is the poor man's pathos, the pathos for everyone, because every human being can act within himself. And one sometimes finds in a maidservant the pathos for which one searches in vain in the existence of the poet.[3]

And in this connection Kierkegaard directed a remark to himself as the wise person who knew full well that simplicity is what counts:

> What the simple religious person does straightforwardly, the simple religiously aware person does only by means of humor. (What is humorous is that, after examining the matter carefully, I still have to

make excuses for doing something that is commanded and recommended as the highest by the lower court, the court of first instance.) This is not to be understood in the sense that his religiousness is humor, but that when he is to state what his religion is, humor is the boundary in relation to which he defines it; humor is the boundary that separates him from the immediate.[4]

It is on this sharp boundary line of humor that Kierkegaard balanced throughout the entirety of this large book. Viewed internally, he balanced between the speculative-dialectical and the immediate. Viewed externally, he balanced between the wise and the simple in an indirectly polemical relation to his times.

Accordingly, at the conclusion he made the following statement to aid the reader's understanding:

> He is a humorist. Satisfied with the conditions of the moment and hoping that something higher will be granted him, he believes that he is especially fortunate, if worse comes to worst, to have been born in precisely this speculative, theocentric century.[5]

Kierkegaard's historical and cultural placement was at once his good fortune and his curse. Like the other cultivated and gifted people, he was caught in the web of speculation, and nothing would have been easier for him than to wrap himself up in it in dignified fashion, as pastors or professors do in their garb, as an external sign of a more profound understanding. But:

> Indeed, if a maidservant wanted me to pay the musicians at her wedding, when she was being married to a manservant, I would gladly do so if I could afford it. And if I had the time, I would gladly dance with her on her wedding day, sharing in the delight of the other happy people. She probably feels no need of a deeper understanding. The idea that I am superior to her because I feel that need is nonsense and is far from my laborious train of thought. Even if I were to find what I sought, I would perhaps not be half so good. But I feel

this need to know what I am doing, the need which at the height of its victory is rewarded with that foolish little difference between the simple person's knowledge of the simple and the wise person's knowledge of it. . . . Yes, everyone who can simply and honestly say that he feels no need for this understanding has of course nothing to reproach himself for. And woe to the person who disturbs him, woe to him who will not leave up to the god what the god requires of each person individually. . . . But when big words are spouted everywhere, in world-historical and systematic fashion, in order to dupe God; when even the clergy is in a hurry to turn its robes inside out so that they might look almost like professorial gowns; when it is everywhere proclaimed that the immediate has been abolished — then it will not arouse the anger of the god if one asks these exalted wise men what they know about this simple matter.[6]

In a number of passages, Kierkegaard presented his idea of the paradox, both in relation to the speculative thinker and in relation to the simple person. The former wants to abolish the paradox, and the latter understands himself and Christianity by means of it. "The simple wise person," Kierkegaard wrote (and here he meant himself),

will then immerse himself in grasping the paradox as paradox and will not involve himself in explaining the paradox by arriving at the understanding that it does not exist. Thus, if the simple wise person talked to a simple person concerning the forgiveness of sins, the simple person would likely say, "But I still cannot grasp the divine mercy that can forgive sins; the more vividly I believe in it the less I can understand it." . . . But the simple wise person would probably say, "It is the same with me. You know that I have had the opportunity to devote a great deal of time to investigating and considering this matter, and yet the sum of all this is, at most, that I grasp that it cannot be understood and that this cannot be otherwise. Look, it's not as if I had any advantage over you: this difference certainly cannot be a source of distress to you or cause you to reflect sadly upon the more laborious circumstances of your own life and upon your perhaps lesser abilities. When viewed as the fruit of my studies, my advantage is enough to make one cry and laugh. But you must never scorn these studies, just as I myself have no regrets concerning them. On the contrary, it pleases me most when I smile about them and then enthusiastically resume the efforts of thinking." . . . But to grasp equality in the strongest possible fashion precisely when one is most strongly rooted in that which differentiates one from others — that is the noble piety of the simple wise person.[7]

In the last volume of his papers, Kierkegaard wrote quite a number of pieces (entitled "About Myself") that essentially were polemics against the cultivated figures of his times. In these pieces, Kierkegaard was not afraid to emphasize his own extraordinary gifts. But regardless of all this secondary attention to his gifts, the passage cited above nonetheless remains the true basis both of his own self-understanding and of our understanding of who he really was. Thus, later in the *Postscript* he could exclaim,

Nor is faith something everyone has, something at which no respectable man of cultivation could halt his development. Although it can be grasped and held fast by the simplest person, it is only all the more difficult for the cultivated person to attain. O wonderful, inspiring Christian humanity: that which is highest is common to all people, and the most fortunately gifted are merely those who have been subjected to the strictest schooling.[8]

In a more serious vein, Kierkegaard added that in modern times, as he described them above, he had to make it difficult to become a Christian, because Christianity is not a doctrine but an existential contradiction and an existential communication. He remarked quite gravely,

This introduction does not make it more difficult for the simple person to become a Christian. It is certainly my view that the utmost efforts to become a Christian also are required of him, just as I believe that no one is doing him a service by making it all too easy. But every essential task of existence pertains equally to every person, and therefore the difficulty is proportionate to the talents and capacities of the individual. . . . To understand that a human being is capable of nothing (the beautiful and profound expression of the relationship to God) is equally difficult for a remarkably talented king and for a poor wretch, and is perhaps more difficult for the king, because he is so easily tempted by the circumstance that he is capable of so much. This is also the case with respect to becoming and being a Christian. And since cultivation and all that sort of thing have made it so extremely easy to be a Christian, it is certainly proper that the single individual, to the best of his limited abilities, should seek to make it difficult — provided, however, that he does not make it more difficult than it is. But the more cultivation and knowledge, the more difficult it is to become a Christian.[9]

Behind all this we can of course glimpse Socrates' dispute with the sophists, though first and foremost we sense Kierkegaard's personal and firsthand experiences, both with the world of the cultivated and the world of the simple people. As a man of the streets, he inhabited both worlds equally. Yet we also see that he did not waver from the viewpoint he set forth in *A Literary Review:* it is the cultivated people, not the common people, that are the problem. Kierkegaard's intention was to awaken and edify, that is, to encourage a genuine and spiritual appropriation. Toward the end of his career, he made the issue even more pointed, insisting that cultivation not only confused a person but also *prevented* the attainment of true awakening. This was why the gigantic figure of Mynster had to be toppled, and why Kierkegaard allowed cultivation and the established church to be dethroned for the sake of the common man. In the *Postscript* we can follow Kierkegaard's progress toward his final campaign.

He spoke of religious suffering, which is a dying-away from immediacy:

I myself am well aware of the feeble figure cut by investigations of everyday matters — matters about which all people, down to the simplest maidservant and common soldier, are well informed. I am aware of how imprudent it is of me to acknowledge the difficulty of this investigation and thereby perhaps reveal my inability to elevate myself even slightly above the intellectual horizon of the lowest class. I am aware of how closely it borders on satire that after spending time and energy for years, one ends up coming no further than to what the stupidest person knows — alas, instead of having expended the same amount of time and energy and having perhaps accomplished something concerning China, Persia, or even astronomy.[10]

And when speaking of his fundamental notion that faith is beyond all reason, Kierkegaard employed a provocative slogan: what is absurd is equally so for everyone, the wise as well as the simple. The absurd is "comparatively most difficult for the person who has much understanding, if one bears in mind that not everyone who has not lost his understanding over Christianity thereby proves that he has it."[11]

Kierkegaard then rounded out and concluded this weighty tome about Christianity's relation to objectivity and subjectivity by asserting yet again what he had focused upon in many earlier passages:

Indeed, if Christianity were a subtle doctrine (in a straightforward sense of what subtlety is) then cultivation would be of straightforward assistance. But in relation to an existential message that paradoxically accentuates what it is to exist, cultivation only helps by increasing the difficulties. Thus, with respect to becoming and continuing to be Christians, the cultivated have only a very ironic advantage over the simple: the advantage that it is more difficult. . . . If Christianity once transformed the form of the world by vanquishing the raw passions of immediacy and ennobling the nations of the earth, it will find in cultivation an equally dangerous opponent. But if this is where the battle is to be joined, it must naturally be fought within the most finely honed categories of reflection. The absolute paradox will certainly be capable of holding its own, because with respect to the absolute, more understanding gets no further than less understanding. On the contrary, both get equally far, the remarkably gifted person slowly, the simple person swiftly. Leave the straightforward praise of cultivation to others, then, and certainly let it be praised. But I would prefer to praise cultivation because it makes it so difficult to become a Christian. For I am a friend of difficulties, and especially of those with this humorous characteristic: that the most cultivated person, having been through the most strenuous exertions, gets essentially no further than the simplest person can. Because the simplest person can indeed become and continue to be a Christian but (both because he does not have any great degree of understanding and also because the sort of life that confronts him causes him to direct his attention outward) he is spared the difficult labors with which the cultivated person, who struggles more and more as his cultivation increases, must sustain his faith. Since becoming and continuing to be a Christian is indeed the highest thing, the task cannot be to reflect upon Christianity but can only be, by means of reflection, to intensify the pathos with which one continues to be a Christian. And this has been the subject of this entire work.[12]

The passages cited from *A Literary Review* and *Concluding Unscientific Postscript* point quite clearly to the task Kierkegaard set for himself throughout all his pseudonymous works as "the unknown" and "the simple wise person": to help his cultivated age to appropriate Christianity. He did this by demonstrating, first, how far the age — with its religious-humanistic views, its speculation, and its philosophy — was from being Christian, and second, by demonstrating how the difficulty in becoming a Christian was rooted in the arrogance that cultivated and gifted people felt concerning things the simple person possessed without difficulty.

The philosophy of existence in the *Postscript* emphasized Christianity's *how* instead of its *what,* thus making Christianity an existential communication. Kierkegaard used the *Postscript* to strike a blow at the speculative thinking of his times, at theological smugness concerning matters of doctrine and systematics. The common man came into the picture here in two ways: both as the equal of the cultivated with respect to what was of essential importance and as the person who had not been corrupted, as had the cultivated, because his capacity for action had not been sapped by reflection. In Kierkegaard's critique of cultivation, the common man thus served both as a foil and as the reinforcement held in reserve: if the cultivated prove impossible to awaken, we can fasten our hope upon the common man.

CHAPTER SEVEN

Reality: Trial by Fire

With the *Postscript* Kierkegaard rounded off his work as an author. His productivity was unprecedented in world literature: in six years he wrote (and thought through) not only the pseudonymous works but also the edifying writings, plus his journals, which by 1847 already take up eight printed volumes. Of course Kierkegaard's contemporaries could not keep abreast of this avalanche of books. People were impressed, and yet they were irritated because he was still so visible on the street and in the theatre. Had these pseudonymous books perhaps been written by several authors? In the *Postscript* Kierkegaard revealed that he had written them all. But as I have shown in Chapter Five, none of them (and most definitely not the members of the various cultural coteries) understood what was taking place before their eyes. In his *Christian Dogmatics* H. L. Martensen dismissed Kierkegaard's attack on speculation as "random thoughts, aphorisms, caprices, and glimpses," and he viewed Kierkegaard's works as "of absolutely no concern" to himself.[1] As we have seen, Martensen's position summarized that of the coteries. People were certainly impressed, but quite confused. Rasmus Nielsen, whose nine lives saw him through all sorts of dialectical changes, immediately saw the point of Kierkegaard's works. Nielsen, however, used his insight into Kierkegaard's work partly to further his polemics against Martensen and partly to promote his own project, i.e., his book *The Faith of the Gospels and Modern Consciousness*. But Nielsen was misled by his own rhetorical talents, and consequently he both understood Kierkegaard and did not understand him. That Nielsen could "live up to his character" (Kierkegaard's term for assuming the ethical responsibilities of one's own role and task in life) was out of the question. Kierkegaard had to put up with a great deal from Nielsen, but Nielsen was the only person with whom he could talk on the dialectical level. And even though, for the sake of his work, Kierkegaard had chosen solitude and silence about his innermost self, he nonetheless had need of a confidant and of someone who could serve as his literary executor and perhaps carry on his cause if he faltered. And it must be admitted that Nielsen, a child of the common people from Funen, came closest to filling the bill.

But otherwise Kierkegaard's works existed as an untenanted island in the sea of his times, a literature within literature. After finishing the *Postscript* he considered retiring to a quiet parsonage. Moreover, after six or seven years of intense writing, his assets had dwindled noticeably. Then along came P. L. Møller,[2] who wrote for *The Corsair* and attacked Kierkegaard in *Gæa*. Indeed, Møller understood more than most people did, and his attitude with respect to Kierkegaard (which was hardly personal, even if they of course did encounter one another) consisted of a mixture of admiration and envy. His attack led to Kierkegaard's challenge that *The Corsair* libel him in its pages, as it had done with other respectable men. M. A. Goldschmidt,[3] the editor of *The Corsair,* quickly accepted this challenge, leading to results Kierkegaard had not anticipated. There is an entire literature concerning this affair that still does not really get to the bottom of it. In all outward appearances Kierkegaard's situation was not unusual, similar to that confronting many other people who have evolved their own views without the security that accompanies an official position or support from some other authority. But herein lay the secret of Kierkegaard's self-understanding, which was now given existential urgency. His abstractions, particularly those concerning the wise and the simple persons, were given experiential content. One could almost say that his understanding of Christianity now became flesh and blood.

The battle with *The Corsair* is the hinge on which Kierkegaard's canon pivots. Now the *Postscript* became not the conclusion of his work as an author but the basis of a new series of writings. As a result of his persecution by *The Corsair* (and the insight into humanity that was the unexpected result of that persecution) Kierkegaard developed a new view of Christianity, in which Christianity was understood as imitation (i.e., the imitation of Christ). This was not a deviation from the original intention of his writings but rather an accentuation of the lines of argument he had set forth earlier. It was a consciously and willfully one-sided corrective to established Christianity, which in the absence of this corrective is an illusion. This was the beginning of the Anti-Climacus period.

But the controversy also shone a new light on the question of the common man and thus gave it decisive significance for Kierkegaard's understanding of Christianity in his contemporary context — and in the context of contemporaneity with Christ. Now Kierkegaard's memories of his home in the 1830s, of the Copenhagen religious awakening movement, of Stormgade, of the religious gatherings out at the limekiln, took on a new relevance. He also saw Jacob Christian Lindberg's situation in a new light, now that he could interpret it on the basis of his own fate. Using passages from Kierkegaard's papers, we will now follow him on his way through the crises, the torment, and the sufferings into which he was thrust by *The Corsair*'s persecution. Out of this crisis and persecution would arise a mature and decisive Kierkegaard, who knew what he wanted and who would steer his course directly toward the battle he was to wage in *The Moment*.

The relationship between Kierkegaard and Goldschmidt was actually very complex. They knew one another and shared a certain common devotion to "the ideal," as it was called in those days. Both were solitary brooders who hid behind wit and satire. Both employed irony as a weapon against their times. In Goldschmidt's novel *Homeless,* one of the characters sets forth the author's position: "If you kept your categories in reasonable order you would know that the satirical is the reverse of the lyrical, that it is a genuine feeling. You would know that in order to avoid sentimentality satire speaks negatively and sometimes, instead of praising a thing, will attack its opposite." Kierkegaard could have said these exact same words. Goldschmidt both understood and admired Kierkegaard, and *The Corsair* published a lengthy and laudatory review of *Either/Or.* Kierkegaard was an interested reader of *The Corsair;* he often discussed articles with the editor and offered suggestions for new subjects. The journal's caricatures of Grundtvig, for example, were surely a source of amusement for Kierkegaard and his peripatetic friend J. L. A. Kolderup-Rosenvinge.[4] The latter privately wrote satirical verse, and a caricature drawing of Grundtvig in *The Corsair* was certainly his inspiration for these lines:

> The national Asa-Tyr,
> The liberal titan of orthodoxy,
> And also an odd fellow,
> Who goes berserk
> At the sound of German and Latin,
> Emptying his brimful drinking horn,
> Full of Braga talk, etc.[5]

This fits in quite nicely with Kierkegaard's own satirical remarks on Grundtvig in his papers. Despite the fact that Kierkegaard was a conservative of sorts, and despite the fact that, like Grundtvig and Lindberg, he loathed liberalism, he was certainly not averse to seeing the cultivated world (which was also the target of his own artillery) come under fire from Goldschmidt and his journal.

Goldschmidt represented the young Denmark that had been inspired by the French Revolution of July 1830 and had now turned against what it called "the men of stagnation." This latter group included such figures as Johan Ludvig Heiberg and in particular Henrik Hertz,[6] who had outraged the younger generation with his book *Moods and Situations* (1839) — which, as it happens, contains a caricature of Kierkegaard in the person of the translator. But in his attack on Orla Lehmann,[7] for example, Goldschmidt also had an eye for the shallow and superficial side of the liberal movement. The development of Danish liberty, Goldschmidt insisted, had been a long-term evolution. Here he was in agreement with Kierkegaard, who was not part of the party of stagnation and whose conservatism was dialectically related to the revolutionary spirit he had praised in *A Literary Review*. (Ibsen later adopted a similar position.)

But neither Hertz nor Goldschmidt realized that behind Kierkegaard's characterization of his times and of the various contending groups there lay a definite religious intention that was linked to the concept of the individual understood as a religious category. Thus Kierkegaard could certainly accept democracy, so long as the individual first became himself vis-à-vis God — and only after that created a fellowship around the democratic idea. This is the basis on which he dismissed the political and social consequences of the July 1830 Revolution (and later the February Revolution of 1848), because they did not lead to this sort of fellowship, but rather channeled the masses into an abstraction called "the public," where ideas were diluted into principles.

And what became of the Revolution of 1848? The common people did not, of course, become passionately connected with an idea that drew its strength from the ethical integrity of the simple individual. A march to the royal palace and the principles of National Liberalism could not propagate the idea of freedom in the people but could certainly win them a few freedoms! This was what Kierkegaard reflected upon, and this was why, as a revolutionary, he preferred the established order — at least as long as it was possible, as he put it, "to breathe some inwardness into it."[8] Kierkegaard viewed aristocratic National Liberalism, with its army of journalists and its command of the press, as a deception of the people, misleading and actually insulting to the common man — who, instead of a revolution, was given a ballot box. Here Kierkegaard was misunderstood yet again: in intellectual matters he could be quite ironically caustic and sarcastic, but in matters concerning the common people he was a completely different person, and this was viewed as an indirect affront to and treason against his class.

People doubted Kierkegaard's sincerity (as they still do), and he was suspected of conducting psychological experiments — which, in good Socratic fashion, he did in fact carry out with his more sophistical contemporaries. But in matters concerning the common man, Kierkegaard's sincerity was absolutely fundamental. This can be explained, in part, by his background and family origins, in part by religious influences, and also by his basic honesty and decency. In matters concerning the common people he was direct, without ulterior motives or condescension. Here he was not a man of reflection, nor was he consumed by skepticism or with self-loathing, as was, for example, Anatole France, who tried to submerge himself in primitiveness. Nor did Kierkegaard adopt his position for the sake of winning popularity; getting himself elected to parliament was the farthest thing from his mind. He had a rare capacity for sharing the thoughts of other people, for entering into their mental universe, whether it was Bishop Mynster or his coachman. Everyone testified to Kierkegaard's ability to provide consolation. Hans Brøchner remarked on this in his memoirs about his twenty years' acquaintance with his distant relative Kierkegaard. (Incidentally, these are the only recollections about Kierkegaard that are fully trustworthy.) And Kierkegaard's letters to his sickly sister-in-law Jette[9] also testify to this ability. He could also be charming and extremely polite. He truly believed what he repeated so often: what matters is to exist for the sake of every person, unconditionally everyone — on the condition, of course, that they do not betray humanity [*Menneske-lighed*] and human equality [*Menneske-Lighed*], whether they do so as a mob of common rabble or, even worse, as a mob of intellectuals and representatives of cultivation.

In *Stages on Life's Way,* from Kierkegaard's aesthetic period, we have the amusing sketch of the maidservants in Frederiksberg Garden. (The passage in question is found in the section on Johannes the Seducer. The seducer has little relation to P. L. Møller but, like other of Kierkegaard's figures, is a fragment of Kierkegaard himself, one of his own possibilities, which he developed as a poet and fantast, to use the resulting existential collisions as a means of furthering his religious-philosophical purpose.) In artistic matters, as in other areas, Kierkegaard could learn from the common people, especially regarding language:

> When one hears a maidservant in conversation with another maidservant, one suddenly gains an insight into something about which one has vainly sought enlightenment in books. A turn of phrase that one has vainly attempted to torture out of one's own brain or sought after in dictionaries (even in the dictionary of the Scientific Society) is heard in passing, uttered by a common soldier who has no idea how wealthy he is. And like a person who walks in the great forest amazed at it all sometimes breaks off a branch, sometimes a leaf, sometimes bends down to a flower, or listens to the call of a bird, one walks among the mass of the people amazed at the marvelous gift of language, picking up in passing first one expression, then another, delighting in it and not being so ungrateful as to forget to whom one is indebted.[10]

Here we have the source of Kierkegaard's remarkable linguistic talent, the richest and most capacious in the Danish language. With his living rhythms and musical nuances, in the pith and clarity of his sentences, he was at equal remove both from normative-academic prose and from arty writing. Even when he delved into the subtlest of abstractions, he preserved the spoken quality and the rhythm of the language. Ever since, as a young man, he had dreamed of writing a work about three figures from popular mythology — Faust, Ahasuerus, and Don Juan — Kierkegaard had been interested in folk tales, both because of their language and because of the insight into the fantasy world of the common people they provide. As we have already noted, Kierkegaard's library contained more than a hundred volumes of fairy tales from many countries — a collection comparable in size to his collection of Danish literature.

In this connection it is strange that he did not seize hold of Hans Christian Andersen, who started out from the same assumptions Kierkegaard made and went on to become a force for renewal of the language. In brilliant fashion Andersen propelled the fairy tale into the age of reflection. With their play of irony and their sensitivity, Andersen's tales were in fact indirect discourse in the style of Kierkegaard and constituted an attack on the Heiberg era. Imaginative elements and artistically retouched naiveté were freighted with symbols or infiltrated by wit and satire, as in "A Leaf from Heaven," "The Nightingale," "The Tinder Box," "The Ugly Duckling," and "The Most Incredible Thing." It is a mystery why a critic of Kierkegaard's stature did not discover a comrade-in-arms in Andersen. Perhaps it was because Kierkegaard's first published work, *From the Papers of One Still Living,* was a curious attack on Andersen. Perhaps Kierkegaard also had his own fixed view of what fairy tales should be, and Andersen's use of veiled irony annoyed him. (Israel Levin mentions this latter point in his remarks on Kierkegaard.[11]) Finally, Kierkegaard probably could not cope with the figure of Andersen when he encountered him on the street: clumsy, loose-limbed, self-absorbed, fishing for "knowledge," but also suddenly revealing himself to be an ironic dialectician, so that one was in doubt as to whether he was merely shamming or striking a pose with all his weaknesses. Andersen produced a brilliant satirical close-up of Kierkegaard as the parrot in "The Galoshes of Good

Fortune," and Kierkegaard must surely have been taken aback by this literary fencing, coming as it did from someone he had considered a sniveler.
Andersen had positioned himself right in the middle of Kierkegaard's field
of interest, the folk tale, but he treated it as Heinrich Heine had the folk
song, combining the honey of naiveté with the sting of irony. Here, in
Andersen, was a genuine instance of the wisely simple person, a role that
Kierkegaard himself loved to play.

Perhaps Kierkegaard's silence was connected in some manner to his
knowledge that it was P. L. Møller (along with Grímur Thomsen)[12] who
had first pointed out Andersen's real genius. In any case, Kierkegaard's relationship with Andersen subsequently improved. Andersen sent him his
fairy tales, including the large two-volume edition of 1845-48 with the
dedication: "*Either* you like my little works *Or* you don't like them. They
are nonetheless sent without *Fear and Trembling,* and that is something, at
any rate"![13] It is quite curious to imagine that these two sons of the common people, the only nineteenth-century Danish writers to achieve world
renown, politely avoided one another because they resembled one another
too closely and had the same battle to wage against the culture of their
times. In his own way, Grundtvig, with his visions of "the people," was in
a similar situation, and all three men could be seen walking on Copenhagen's Østergade. As far as the cultivated people of the time were concerned, there was something ridiculous about all three of them.

Kierkegaard owned only a couple of books by Andersen, while he
owned six volumes of stories (as well as the Ossian translations) by Steen
Steensen Blicher,[14] a writer from the faraway precincts of Jutland.
Kierkegaard valued Blicher far more highly than he did Andersen, and he
often mentioned Blicher's work, both in his published writings and in his
papers. Kierkegaard found Blicher's sketches of the common people captivating and refreshing in their credibility and accuracy, their precise psychology and sure artistry. Perhaps this was due to the influence of Kierkegaard's father, who had often told his son about his home on the heath of
West Jutland. Moreover, one never saw Blicher on Copenhagen's Østergade, where Kierkegaard and the other strolling geniuses kept the pot
boiling. Both the theme and the melancholy tone of a collection of poems like Blicher's *Birds of Passage* (1838) appealed to Kierkegaard. In his

polemical book against Andersen, Kierkegaard had emphasized Blicher's "native originality." Here, in Blicher, was the unity of a "fundamental poetic tone that echoes in the inner ear of the soul, a tone that is individual yet rooted in the common people, *and* a fantasy-laden expression of a popular-idyllic image that is illuminated by mighty flashes of summer lightning."[15]

But let us now move away from this secondary material, important though it is as background, and turn to entries in Kierkegaard's journals and papers from the period of his clash with *The Corsair*. In this connection we will pay particular attention to his remarks concerning the common man, a matter of ever-increasing importance for Kierkegaard and one that determined the trajectory and goal of his final years. Kierkegaard's populist attitude toward the individuals who constituted what he called the simple class of people was inextricably linked with the *Corsair* affair. We have noted Kierkegaard's battle against the coteries of culture, both the old conservative cliques and those of the new liberal observance. Kierkegaard was close to Lindberg, and the high praise he had for him in the *Postscript* was aimed not only at Grundtvig and his party but also at conservative clerics, who remembered the quarrelsome Lindberg all too well. With respect to Mynster, whose greatness Kierkegaard admired and toward whom he felt filial piety, Kierkegaard assumed an attitude of armed neutrality. Martensen had been Kierkegaard's special target, however, and it was thus no surprise when no one came rushing to Kierkegaard's defense during the *Corsair* affair. Instead, people joined in the general laughter with malicious glee, mocking the defenseless Kierkegaard, who, confronted with a crowd of scoffers like a swarm of bees, was unable to assert his superiority.

But true to his purpose, during this period Kierkegaard also aired his differences with Copenhagen's religiously awakened circles, including the various followers of Grundtvig and Lindberg, known collectively as "the old-fashioned orthodox" or "the holy." In *The Concept of Anxiety* he wrote:

The so-called holy people often tend to be the objects of the world's mockery. Their own explanation of this is that the world is wicked. But this is not entirely true. If a "holy" person is unfree in relation to

89

his piety (that is, if he lacks inwardness), from a purely aesthetic point of view he is comical, and to this extent the world is right to laugh at him. . . . One hears such a holy person quietly beating time, as it were, just like a person who cannot dance but is nevertheless capable of following the rhythm — even if he is never fortunate enough to get in step. Thus the "holy" person knows that the religious is absolutely commensurable, that it is not something that belongs only to certain occasions and moments, but is rather something you can always have with you. But at the very moment that he is about to make it commensurable, he is not free. He can be seen quietly beating time, and despite this effort, he errs and goes astray with his heavenward gaze, his folded hands, etc. This is why this sort of individual is so anxious about everyone who does not have this training, that in order to reassure himself he must resort to these grandiose remarks about how the world hates pious people.[16]

This passage is a bit abstract and was destined for later revision, but all the same it is one of the many passages in which Kierkegaard attacked the Christian self-deception that can result from involvement in religious movements and group meetings, instead of being an individual person, who in the absence of the support of movements and groups can only rely upon God's mercy. Thus, even though they could see from his edifying discourses that he was somehow one of them, the religiously awakened looked upon Kierkegaard with a certain skepticism. Kierkegaard was among those who took up the cause of edification and awakening, but Lindberg and Bone Falch Rønne, after all, were people one could understand. They had authority and directness; they led the battle against state Christianity and palpable persecution. But this little Magister Kierkegaard? On the other hand, he was undeniably a friend of the people like that other magister, the great Magister Lindberg, and it was known that you could talk with him freely about matters both ordinary and profound. But you never saw him make fiery speeches at assemblies. Wasn't there something a bit odd about him, something comical, as in the pictures of him in *The Corsair*? And his trouser legs: *were* they of equal length? Let's have a look tomorrow.

Kierkegaard wrote,

> This is actually how I am treated in Copenhagen. I am regarded as a
> kind of Englishman, a half-mad eccentric, with whom every damned
> one of us, from highest aristocrats to guttersnipes, imagine we can
> have a bit of fun. My work as an author, that enormous productivity,
> the intensity of which, it seems to me, could move stones, the indi-
> vidual segments of which (not to mention the totality) not one living
> writer can compete with: this writing is regarded as a sort of hobby,
> like fishing and such. Those who could produce something them-
> selves envy me and remain silent. And the others understand noth-
> ing. I do not receive the support of a single word from reviews and
> the like. I am plundered by small-time prophets in foolish lectures at
> religious meetings and the like. But mention me by name? No, that
> isn't necessary.[17]

There were scores of similar comments over the years, in a rising tone
that sometimes had the sound of a tortured cry. He had encountered
something he had never dreamt of, and he was defenseless. Kierkegaard
had expected that after retaliating for his own attack, *The Corsair* would
have stopped, especially after both Goldschmidt and P. L. Møller had gone
abroad. But the repercussions became worse and worse. Nothing amused
Copenhagen so much as this making sport of the learned and ridiculous
magister. And not even 1848 and the increased attention to national issues
could silence the city's gossipers. But what had he done? He wrote,

> I love my native land. It is true that I have not gone to fight in the
> war, but I believe that I have served my country in another way, and I
> believe that I am correct in thinking that Denmark must seek its
> strength in spirit and intelligence. I am proud of my mother tongue
> whose secrets I know, the mother tongue that I treat more lovingly
> than a flautist does his instrument.
>
> I know that I have sincerely loved every person. Even if many
> have treated me as their enemy, I have had no enemy. I have . . . never
> known a time when thoughts and ideas would not come to me. But I

have known something else. If, on my way home from a walk, which is when I meditate and gather ideas, . . . if some poor person along the way had addressed me, and if in my excitement over my ideas I had not had time to talk with him, then when I reached home it would be as though everything was gone, and I would sink into the most frightful spiritual scruples at the thought that what I had done to that person, God could do to me. If, on the other hand, I took the time to talk with the poor person and listen to him, this never happened to me.[18]

Here we see the religious context in which Kierkegaard placed his behavior and his attitude in everyday life. He returned to the line of argument from the *Postscript:*

Oh, what a consolation, what a relief it is if communication is not related to the differences between one person and another. When one does not focus upon these differences, one has the consolation of perhaps being able to find in the common man an honest person who can and will understand. . . . It is in fact precisely among ordinary people that the greatest strengths are to be found. At first glance, one might be tempted to view this as the suffering in Christ's life, which in a sense it was: that he had to seek his disciples among the common people. Oh, but what a consolation it was for him, compelled as he was to feel his heterogeneity with the established order so deeply, that the common man was nonetheless related to him as a possibility.

But the person whose communication has to do with the differences between one person and another is cut off from this final, consoling access. A presentation in which the dialectical element is the very point cannot address itself to the man of the common people. In his search he is thus limited to the established order. He must look for the necessary talents and abilities — and also for the specific quality of honesty. What wonder, then, if he searches in vain? Because this latter quality is found most readily in a man of the common people, who makes very few demands of life and has not been initiated into the dangers of cultivation.[19]

Kierkegaard reflected upon the unreasonable situation in which he was placed and discovered something that made sense from a religious point of view. People preach about the rich man and about Lazarus,

Thus, they preach that a person must be merciful. But I almost never see any reference to the double danger[20] here. Because if you are truly merciful and have money to give the poor; and more than that, if you truly have a heart in your breast; if you are kind to every poor and needy person; . . . if you are willing to receive the greeting of the poor and to greet them in turn in friendly fashion (not aloofly, in the third person *en passant,* but affectionately, as one greets an acquaintance); if you are willing to speak with the poor man on the street and willing to permit yourself to be addressed by him on the street: in brief, if you are truly tender and merciful, then you will see that unless you enjoy extraordinary respect as someone quite special, you will be laughed at and mocked for doing this. . . . The frivolous crowd will laugh every time they see you standing there talking with a poor person. And if (perhaps with the help of the press, which of course is campaigning for the well-being of the simple class of people!) this comes to be common knowledge about you, it may end with the mob insulting you. Shrewd people, who seek finite goals, will view you as mad, not so much because you give your money away like this as because in this way you undermine and lose the public respect you enjoy. Because poor people, of course, are not always tactful enough to avoid placing you in peculiar situations now and then. And the more distinguished people, who of course have a bit more understanding of things, will sense in a fleeting glance the awkwardness of the situation and will hurriedly avert their eyes so as to avoid seeing you — and then pass by with the entire panoply of worldly honor and esteem, the objects of the startled crowd's deference. . . . I have seen this happen, and however much I am sometimes disgusted with existence when I think of it, I am comforted by one thing: that by having seen it and having seen it so close at hand, I learn to understand Christianity. Fortunately, things have often worked out like this for me: I have experienced something, a situation I myself have brooded and thought

93

about, and only later have I come to the realization that this is of course what Christianity teaches.[21]

Here, and in a series of reflections that followed this entry, Kierkegaard interpreted his own situation as analogous to that of Christ. What had previously been abstract reflections, he now began to understand as real. And the idea of contemporaneity with Christ was now given a firm foundation in the idea of imitation. But Kierkegaard nonetheless paused to reflect on this important point:

> One thing must be noted, however, in connection with contemporaneity with Christ and with making it into the criterion for being a Christian. The point I have developed in various writings about contemporaneity as the criterion is poetically, historically, and ethically absolutely true, and it thus has its validity in this respect and with respect to Christ insofar as he was an actual historical person. But Christ is also a dogmatic reality. Herein lies the difference. His death is of course the atonement. At this point, the category changes qualitatively. From the death of a witness to the truth I am to learn to will to die, as he did, for the truth. . . . But with respect to Christ's death, I cannot will this in the same way, because Christ's death is not a task for imitation, but is the atonement. . . . Thus the situation is not a simple and straightforward one in which Christ is the Exemplar and I ought only to will to be like him. For one thing, I of course need his help in order to be able to resemble him. And for another, insofar as he is the Savior and Reconciler of the human race, I of course cannot resemble him.[22]

Kierkegaard subsequently added the following comment:

> There must be an end to all the spoiled-child nonsense about Christianity satisfying the deepest longings, etc. No, only "the anguished conscience in struggle and extremity"[23] can help one dare to will to have anything to do with Christianity. Otherwise Christianity gives — and must give — offense.[24]

He rounded out these reflections with some lines that point forward from *A Literary Review* and the *Postscript* toward *The Moment:*

> To be in a position to live for an idea, to be able to expend all one's time on it, is indeed closer to relating oneself to the ideal — although, of course, when the ideal is Christ, there is the infinite qualitative difference between him and the person who comes nearest to him. But the people, the great mass of people who must spend most of their time in menial tasks, earning the necessities of life — with respect to them, it would be a terrible thing to jack up the price. In their case, the humane thing is of course to provide consolation and gentleness, because the most fundamental worry and concern of these people can certainly be the pain caused by their inability to live for something higher. Truly, truly, this too is something I have felt and recognized, and it has always been a source of inexpressible inspiration to me that, before God, it is just as important to be a maidservant, if that is what one is, as to be the most brilliant genius. This is also the source of my almost exaggerated sympathy for the simple class of people, the common man. And therefore I can become depressed and sad because they have been taught to laugh at me, thus depriving themselves of the one person in this country who has loved them most sincerely. No, it is the cultivated and well-to-do class — if not the aristocrats, then at any rate the aristocratic bourgeoisie — they must be targeted. That is where the prices in the salon must be jacked up.[25]

Here, in 1849, we have one of the sources of the vehemence of the *Moment* campaign, and we can see the social intention behind the religious one. Kierkegaard often felt tired to death of this daily mockery at the hands of the mob and the guttersnipes on the one hand, and the cool superiority of his peers on the other. He noted that his peers avoided him whenever they could, in order to avoid exposing themselves to taunts and insults:

> [I]t seems to me that it cannot be long before death makes an end of the matter. And indeed, a dead man is precisely what Copenhagen

and Denmark need if there is ever to be an end to this infamous meanness, envy, and mockery. Therefore I am not complaining, even though it might seem to be a hard fate that I — who, had I lived in any other country, would have earned a great fortune, would have been counted among the most eminent geniuses, and would have enjoyed wide and pervasive influence — by having been born in a demoralized provincial town, have quite predictably achieved status as a sort of local madman, known and insulted by (quite literally) every guttersnipe, even by convicted criminals. And all the while the envious upper classes were quietly amused and enjoyed their triumph. . . . For three years everyone has maintained absolute silence while this has continued daily. . . . Only a dead man can stop and avenge such infamy, in which an entire nation is more or less implicated. But all you who have suffered will be avenged! . . . Retribution is coming![26]

In Kierkegaard's papers from 1847, we have a couple of momentary glimpses into his situation at that time:

While mob-like behavior makes fun of me, . . . aristocratic envy looks on with approval. They do not begrudge me that. . . . Incidentally, this sort of irritating mistreatment is among the most painful of things. Everything else comes to an end, after all, but this never ceases. To sit in church, and to have a couple of louts impudently sit next to me in order to stare at my trousers and carry on a mocking conversation so loudly that every word can be heard.[27]

For example, when I have sought recreation by driving twenty or thirty miles away . . . , and I step down from the coach, and it happens that I am received by a mocking assembly, and some of those present are even nice enough to call me names: it has a very powerful effect on my physical well-being. Or when I have walked a long way on quiet paths, lost in thought, and then suddenly encounter three or four louts out there, where I am quite alone, and these fellows take to calling me names: it has an enormously powerful effect on my health. I do not have the physical strength to fight, and I know of nothing that has so depressed my spirit as scenes like this. I have the ability to make any man listen to reason, but one cannot talk to a crude boor, much less three of them who have been given their marching orders by the press.[28]

There are many such personal remarks which, taken together, give a harrowing picture of the daily pains that reinforced Kierkegaard's belief in the view of man contained in the Gospels. As his reflections deepened, Kierkegaard descended to a profound and unchangeable constant in human nature, one that is always there, surprising even the best of us, though usually only revealed in time of war: the problem of evil, and not least the evil of good people. He saw deeply into an aspect of the subterranean life of the soul that he had never seen before, specifically the problem of evil visited upon defenseless persons. Of course, when it senses the presence of power or authority, this same evil behaves itself and becomes servile and humble. Hans Christian Andersen, who indeed experienced situations similar to Kierkegaard's, but who had protectors, touched upon this in "The Ugly Duckling." Both men were odd, and were therefore pushed around. But Kierkegaard experienced it to an extent and depth unparalleled in Denmark, either before or since, with perhaps Lindberg as the only exception. The mob quickly discovered that Kierkegaard was fair game, that the cultivated world had dropped him, and that by their silence the elite had maliciously delivered him up for daily whipping.

Not surprisingly, Kierkegaard experienced a Christ-like situation, not merely abstractly and dialectically, but also existentially, almost in his very body. Kierkegaard experienced the position Christianity had had in the world when it had not been backed up with power, and he learned that when Christianity is backed up by power it is an illusion. In the fire of these experiences were forged the weapons with which he would fearlessly attack his times. As an alarming corrective to the Christianity of his era, he would insist upon the imitation of Christ as the one facet of Christianity without which the proclamation of all the other facets made a fool of God. And to this must be added the suffering of a person of spirit who wishes to assert an idea based only on the depth of his or her being, without the backing of parties or coteries. The results will be persecution, isolation, and (from those who are clever enough to evaluate the situation) silence — the silence of those who do not want to risk their office and their authority by supporting such an individual, often a silence in which envy is camouflaged as self-respect.

> Professor Heiberg and company will say something like this: "Magister Kierkegaard himself is to blame for the whole affair. Why hasn't he allied himself with us and lived in the concealment of high rank?" . . . And it is by courts such as this that my efforts are to be judged! If Heiberg only understood me, if he understood how I quite literally and deliberately thwart myself (in order, it must be noted, that I not serve the truth by means of illusions) he would immediately view me as mad.[29]

> But why must I be forced to be a distinguished person? Strange. I have quite specifically wanted *not* to be distinguished, and by the entire manner in which I live, precisely by being willing to associate with every person, I have made myself the object of the displeasure of distinguished people. The mob is suddenly egged on against me, and I am denounced as proud. And this is precisely how I am forced, finally, into the posture of a distinguished person, which I must adopt simply in order to protect myself from the vulgarity of the mob. Now the people with whom I used to associate as an equal are becoming angry again.[30]

And yet in a lonely moment, he could write,

> Alas, yes, I admit it, it has concerned me very much, and very intensely, that I recognize every poor person who recognizes me, that I remember to greet every servant to whom I had the slightest connection, that I remember that he was ill the last time I saw him, that I then ask him how he is now. Never in my life, not even when I was most preoccupied with an idea, have I ever been so busy that I did not have time to stand still if I were being addressed by a poor per-

son. Is this a crime, then? I would have been ashamed before God and would have saddened my own soul if I had become so self-important that I had to say that "other people" did not exist for me.[31]

During the entire period from 1846 to 1855 there was a certain uniformity to all of Kierkegaard's remarks concerning his painful situation and its relationship to the common man. But in the course of his reflections his remarks gradually take on clarity. One gets the feeling that they are being assembled and arranged as fuel for an approaching situation, a bonfire, an explosion.

Kierkegaard saw clearly the connections between *A Literary Review,* the *Postscript,* and his situation as the martyr of the moment:

In my writings, the conflict, the world-movement, is between two concepts: *the interesting* and *the simple.* The times have gone astray and continue to be carried away by the interesting. The movement to the simple should be made. Therefore I possessed the interesting to an extraordinary degree (it was what the times required). . . . By falsifying my task I could have become the hero and idol of the moment. If I had done so, I would indeed have abandoned the movement toward the simple and would have converted all my power into the interesting and into the moment. I remained true to my task, understood in the eternal sense. I became the martyr of the moment, and this is precisely the proof that I remained true to the task.[32]

The events of 1848 did not result in revolutionary changes with respect to the established church in Denmark. Kierkegaard's task was religious, and (unlike Grundtvig) he was not interested in the external circumstances of religion, but only in the existential dimension. The established order, to which he was otherwise attached, came to seem less and less tenable to him, even if a number of years had to pass before he denounced it, in the wake of Mynster's death:

"The established order" is on the whole an entirely un-Christian concept. But it is even more ridiculous to hear the establishment boast in comparing itself to "the sects," for despite everything there is infinitely more Christian truth in the errors of the sects than in the torpor, drowsiness, and inertia of the established order. . . . But nowadays a sect is always superior to the established order because it has the awakening of truth — that is, it has the truth that lies in being "awakened," even if what the sect views as truth is untruth and error.[33]

The last two lines in the passage cited above point forward, toward "the truth that lies in being 'awakened'." This truth is quite separate from all the exaggeration of *The Moment* campaign, and it formed the real basis for that campaign — a point we will discuss subsequently. First of all, however, it requires an honest attitude, so that the commands of the New Testament are coupled with the admission that a person is incapable of living up to them.

One of the fundamental concepts of Kierkegaard's philosophy is the concept of *actuality,* which was the fruit of his battle with the subjectivism and the systematic objectivism of the times, but which was also the product of Kierkegaard's direct relationship to existence and his own age:

"To come to actuality" also means willing to exist for every person, to the extent that one is capable of doing so. . . . From a Christian point of view I am not permitted existentially to ignore one single person. I am permitted to ignore an anonymous publicist, the public, and all such fantastic entities, but no actual person. . . . There is a collision here: from a Christian point of view, one is not permitted to ignore one single solitary person, but if one is not willing to ignore the multitude, one incites them against oneself.[34]

But Kierkegaard's self-understanding was growing:

This mistreatment has also enriched me dialectically [by showing me] Christianity's essential collision with the world, something that otherwise would have escaped me, overly concerned as I was with inner sufferings. . . . Here again, it is really my relationship to God that has to be developed. When one struggles with a person who in

the ideal sense is actually one's superior or one's equal, the relationship to God is obscured or completely forgotten. But no struggle is
so calculated to develop a person in a godly way as a struggle in
which he is the stronger, and in which, nonetheless, in another
sense, the weaker party [i.e., the crowd] is the stronger.[35]

But Kierkegaard returned to the continuing source of his greatest pain,
the fact that the common man, who had been his friend, now laughed at
him along with the others. Now the common man, too, thought this odd
person was comical. Is he really in his right mind? He talks with people so
much, and Mynster and Martensen never do that. But they of course oc-
cupy high offices. They have amounted to something. But this odd magister, could he perhaps become a pastor? But of course he has money, so he
can afford to behave as crazily as he wishes. Using his reflective capacity
for free association, Kierkegaard interpreted the train of thought that lay
behind the smirks and the embarrassment and the stolen glances down at
his trousers. Yes, it was true — he hadn't made anything of himself. And
he had probably ruined his chances for any sort of appointment. He had
tried to drop a few hints about a position at the pastoral seminary, but both
Mynster and Johan Nicolai Madvig had gotten rid of him. He had continually spoken about being the individual; now he had become one in the
highest existential sense of the term — "the incarnation of his category,"
he would have said with his ever-present smile. Amount to something or
stick to something; he had made his choice, and he felt no envy for those
who had backers, who held offices, who wore disguises. He had long ago
settled accounts with all of them, with one exception: Mynster. But as
Kierkegaard took note of how the head of the old establishment had now
learned to adapt to the new, post-1849 establishment, this idol too was beginning to appear hollow.

Now Kierkegaard was really alone, God's clown among men, the
scourge of God. The moment had not yet arrived. He knew well that in
the snake pit of his times, one thing could protect him and save him: to
disdain people, to withdraw and laugh at the stupidity of the mob and at
the silly pageant of culture. But here, behind all of his secondary attributes
such as talent and genius, we see the first lineaments of Kierkegaard's true

101

greatness. Here, in the hell of his suffering, he triumphed over disdain and held fast to love, and above all, love for the common man, who knew not what he did, misled as he was by the pastors and by the press. Cultivated folk knew very well what they were doing, and therefore, indeed the day would surely come when he would search in vain for ten righteous men among them. He had addressed these cultivated people in their own language in an attempt to rescue them from leveling and illusions, so that they could honestly say at least Yes or No, Either or Or, so that they could choose perdition or salvation with the awareness of what was at stake. Still, perhaps one ought to be more hard-hitting, as Lindberg had been in his day. No matter: Kierkegaard the quarrelsome figure, the scandal journalist, was ready.

Toward the end of 1849 his many remarks about the common man came to be characterized by a concealed social pathos:

> Oh, the manner in which I lived with the common man: in this entire generation there is perhaps not one single person who could do it. And how few are they who understand the common man and understand the extent to which contact with him is usually based upon the hardheartedness and cruelty of class distinctions and respectability. And then to have this contact denied me, to have it regarded as a ridiculous exaggeration, so that I can no longer do anything for the common man, because I exist for him as a sort of half-mad figure.[36]

He gave this picture of his comings and goings on the streets of Copenhagen:

> There is nevertheless something indescribably sad about my life situation. I wanted to live with the simple man. It was indescribably satisfying to me to be friendly and kind and attentive and sympathetic to precisely that social class that is all too neglected in the so-called "Christian state." What I could accomplish was in many ways insignificant. . . . Let me take an example, and I have scores of them. An oldish-looking woman from Amager sits in the arcade selling fruit. She has an elderly mother for whom I have occasionally done a

little. When I greet her, I have not really done anything. Nevertheless it pleased her, it cheered her up, that every morning a person whom she might regard as fortunate in life came by and never forgot to say good morning and occasionally also to speak a few words with her. And indeed I was precisely the sort of idler that the Christian state needs if it is ever to do the least bit to right the outrageous wrong of its existence. For everyone grasps for the higher and more distinguished social positions, and as soon as they get there, what do they care about the common man of the people? There is a need for an idler of this sort — or for many of them. . . . How heartening it is in so many ways for the class of people who must otherwise stand and wait in anterooms, who are hardly permitted to say a single word — how heartening it is that there is one person whom they continually see on the street, a person whom they can approach and talk with freely.[37]

Kierkegaard revealed his social pathos with the following lines:

But the common man, whom I loved! It was my greatest joy to express at least a bit of love for my neighbor. When I beheld that abominable social condescension toward the lesser classes, then I could dare say to myself: "At least I do not live like that." It was a consolation for me to be able to mitigate things a bit in that respect when it was possible. . . . That is the way I was made. So it saddens me indescribably when I have to bear the derision of the common man.[38]

Kierkegaard varied this theme many times in his journals and papers throughout 1850 and 1851. Then, toward the end of 1851, the idea that the Christianity of the New Testament does not exist made its appearance. But he was very hesitant about it:

Yet it is always dangerous to insist too much upon the distinction between true and false Christians, because if one cites heroism and the like as the hallmark of the former, it can so easily become paganism. Therefore I have also always insisted that Christianity is properly for poor people, who perhaps toil and grind all day and can barely earn enough to live on. The more advantageous one's position, the more difficult it is to become a Christian, because reflection can so easily take the wrong direction. I had also long wanted to preach to the common man. But then the vulgar press did everything it could to present me to the common man as a madman, so I had to abandon that wish for a while, but I will certainly return to it.[39]

In this connection came a remark that reminds one of Lindberg:

Therefore I never forget that for Christianity it is just as possible to be a shoemaker, a tailor, or a manual laborer as to be the most learned and intelligent man. Yes, as a rule the church must always expect its salvation from a layman, precisely because he is closer to being ethically ordained.[40]

Subsequent passages from 1852 and 1853 do not change the picture we have already formed, and what he wrote in 1854 is the same as what he had written earlier:

I cannot stop liking the common man, and this despite the fact that in this country the despicable press does everything to confuse him with respect to me and to embitter me about what I had loved so unutterably, what had been for me the most refreshing rest from intellectual labor — to live in the company of the common man.[41]

And later:

I love the common man. The assistant professors [*Docenterne*] are an abomination to me. It is precisely the assistant professors who have demoralized the race. Everything would be better if things were allowed to be as they truly are: the few who are truly in service of the idea, or even higher, in God's service — and after them, the people. But the infamy is that these scoundrels, this gang of thieves, has inserted itself between the former group and the people. Giving the appearance that they, too, are servants of the idea, they betray the true servants and confuse the people, all for the sake of wretched worldly advantages. If there were no hell, one would have to be created in order to punish the assistant professors, whose crime is precisely of the sort that cannot very well be punished in this world.[42]

Kierkegaard continued this train of thought with the following:

Much would be gained if only those few individuals who actually relate themselves to spirit could come to exert influence upon the common man. But it is precisely the intermediate group which is the misfortune of human existence.[43]

This was so because

God's Word must be proclaimed to the people. . . . "The people" always constitute the health that can engender something good. Whatever has amounted to something in the world and whatever derives from anything that has amounted to something is generally already weakened, probably even corrupted. . . . Therefore, for this reason and for many others, the Word of God must be proclaimed to the people.[44]

After a series of passages from *A Literary Review,* the *Postscript,* and the *Corsair* affair we have now come to 1855, and throughout these eight or nine years we have observed the same tendency: against cultivation and the bourgeois upper class, and in favor of the people. In the years up to 1848 and its immediate aftermath, Kierkegaard was more in step with the European revolution than anyone else in Denmark. He was more "social" than he was "liberal" or "national," and to this extent one can say that he was on the same wavelength as Marx and Engels (or, in Denmark, Frederik Dreier).[45] But Kierkegaard was situated closer to the practical, everyday life of the people than were these others, and he clung to his faith in the people even during their attack on him. As we have seen, the "common man" was a crucial term for him. It was for the sake of the common man that

Kierkegaard carried on his campaign in *The Moment,* and the last words he ever wrote for publication were a salutation to the common man.

Nonetheless, from the very beginning he turned his back on mass political uprisings unless they were built on a revolutionary foundation that required each individual in the mass to relate himself, as an individual, passionately to a shared and unifying idea. The purpose of this requirement was to prevent the individual from surrendering to mass suggestion. For Kierkegaard the mass, as such, was always untruth. He remained shackled to the pillar he called "the individual." Kierkegaard's task during that decade of great political and social movements was to propose both a worldly and a religious corrective as absolute necessities. He had a better eye than anyone else for how the journalists and the demagogues of progress had used the power of mass suggestion to deceive the people into shirking all responsibility, as well as their own originality, in order to lure them into the trap of dictatorship (to use a modern expression). The same was true regarding his central concern, religion and the church. Here, too, he turned against demagoguery. This was the point of the *Moment* campaign: the pastors were weaving the fabric of religious twaddle, and in so doing they were betraying the gospel in order to satisfy the so-called "deepest longings" of the human spirit. Here we recall Kierkegaard's remark: "There must be an end to all the spoiled-child nonsense about Christianity satisfying the deepest longings." He considered this matter in his book on Adler, where he wrote, "One does not become a Christian by being religiously seized by something higher, and not every outpouring of religious emotion is a Christian outpouring."[46]

Thus Kierkegaard could certainly have agreed with Marx ("Religion is the opiate of the people") because this was precisely the point of the *Moment* campaign. But he surely would have shrugged his shoulders at Marx's anthropology, which, like that of Hegelianism, is a death sentence for existence and thus also for freedom. Therefore, unlike Marx, Kierkegaard fought on two fronts. He was even more opposed to the objectivism of systems than to subjectivism. Every false anthropology — religious subjectivism or Marxian objectivism — always meets its nemesis. This has been demonstrated by the historical fate both of Western European subjectivism and Eastern European objectivism.

But to return to our text and to the matter at hand, the selected passages we have examined demonstrate a coherent vision, first in the form of abstract reflection and thereafter as a commentary on the practice of the imitation of Christ. This coherent vision amplifies tendencies that begin early in the pseudonymous literature and point toward the *Moment* campaign. Many people have been confused by the consciously journalistic form of Kierkegaard's *Moment* campaign and have been unable to discern the connection between it and the *Corsair* affair, especially as the latter relates to the question of the common man. In this connection we should note that the use made of the *Moment* campaign by certain amateur freethinkers in order to further their own agenda has revealed their shallow grasp of the Kierkegaardian project. Kierkegaard was more radical (and more socially aware) than naturalism's pseudo-radicals, who were in general nothing more than disguised National Liberals.

Kierkegaard leapt from abstractions into reality, subjecting his ideas to a trial by fire, when (as he repeatedly emphasized) he voluntarily exposed himself to the attack by *The Corsair.* He summed up the value of the battle with *The Corsair* in providing a perspective on his situation as follows:

> For me the result [was] the satisfaction of having been true to myself and to my idea, of not having shrunk back from any consequence, but having dared to the utmost. . . . When I gave up being an aesthetic writer and thus lost the support that aesthetic writing provided with its guarantee of indirectness of communication, I nonetheless guaranteed support for indirect communication in another fashion: namely by creating this opposition to myself. If I had not taken this step, I would have utterly avoided the *double* danger connected with Christianity, so that I would have continued to think of the difficulties involved with Christianity as being only interior to the self. This was my own education and development. As an author, I have gotten a new string on my instrument and have become capable of producing notes that I would never have dreamt of otherwise. I have come to "actuality" in a much stricter sense of the term.[47]

Kierkegaard subsequently repeated this point more directly:

How I have suffered from the persecution of the vulgar mob and from human ingratitude! Yet truly, without it I would have completely missed one side of Christianity. To undertake a high-minded action out of love for others and to see it rewarded in this way; to have the experience of being declared an egotist precisely because I was not self-serving; to see all the egotism that is the basic driving force in society; to see this egotism united in declaring me an egotist at the very moment when I was unconditionally sympathetic to others — yes, that was really enough to drive me mad. Fortunately, I was well tutored in Christianity from my childhood on. That helped. But truly I also came to know Christianity from the ground up.[48]

This is something Kierkegaard emphasized frequently: the *Corsair* affair made the true Christian dimension of things clear to him, and he came in particular to understand that those who cried "Hosanna!" to Christ on Palm Sunday were the same people who cried "Give us Barabbas!" on the evening of Maundy Thursday: the common people.

Attacks upon Kierkegaard (or, rather, the misunderstandings of him) have often focused especially on the matter of subjectivity being truth. Even in Kierkegaard's day, critics used a careless reading of the *Postscript* to conclude that he was some sort of individualist:

See, I have not been understood at all in this respect either. All of the more profound thinkers . . . agree that evil is to be found in isolated subjectivity. Objectivity is what saves. This, in turn, has long since become a slogan, and of course every university student knows that I am an isolated individuality. Ergo, I am all but evil, "pure negativity, without seriousness, etc." Oh, profound confusion! No, the entire concept of objectivity that has been made into the principle of salvation merely feeds the illness, and the fact that it is praised as the cure demonstrates just how fundamentally irreligious the times are. . . . No, it is precisely in order to put an end to subjectivity in its untruth that we must go right through to "the individual" — vis-à-vis God. . . . In these areas it takes a fortunate genius . . . to understand things correctly. I am not boasting about anything. It is quite true that isolated subjectivity, in the sense in which the times use the term, is also an evil, but a cure by means of "objectivity" is not one whit better. Salvation must come through subjectivity, that is, through God as the infinitely compelling subjectivity.[49]

In these lines, Kierkegaard denied that the controversial principle of subjectivity exists as a psychological category that ethics can convert into some sort of humanistic truth-seeking, defining it instead as a religious and Christian category — the category that formed the basis of his position during the painful *Corsair* affair.

During this journey through passages from several years of Kierkegaard's works and papers, I have not consulted or referred to the works he wrote on the basis of his new experiences: *Works of Love, The Sickness Unto Death,* and *Practice in Christianity.* Nor have I referred to Kierkegaard's retrospective rationalization, *The Point of View for My Work as an Author.* He did not dare publish this latter work, and quite properly so, as it would only have added to the confusion and opposition he faced. Rather, as with so many other things, he put this work aside to await understanding by a subsequent generation. Let us conclude this chapter by letting Kierkegaard speak to us yet again, this time from *The Point of View,* where he summarizes his thoughts on a topic that accompanied him (and has accompanied us) for quite a few years.

I took genuine Christian satisfaction in daring on Monday to put into practice a little bit, at least, of what one weeps about on Sunday, when the pastor preaches about it and weeps over it — and about which, sure enough, we laugh on Monday. I took genuine Christian satisfaction in the fact that even if no one else did so, there was definitely one person in Copenhagen whom any poor person could freely address and converse with on the street; that even if no one else did it, there was one person who, regardless of what company he kept on other occasions, did not slink away, but acknowledged every maidservant and manservant, every day laborer he knew. I took genuine Christian satisfaction in the fact that even if there was no one else, there was at least one person who (some years before existence

taught the human race the lesson yet again) made an attempt at putting into practice a bit of the doctrine about loving one's neighbor —
and, alas, in so doing obtained a frightful insight into the extent to which Christendom is an illusion. . . .[50]

Truly, one thing I have never been is aristocratic, not even the least bit. And, being myself of humble origin, I have loved the common man, or what is called the simple class of people. This is something I know I have done, for I took a sad delight in doing so. And yet it is precisely these people who have been incited against me and who have been led to believe that I was aristocratic. Had I actually been aristocratic, this would never have happened to me. See, this is exactly in keeping with the Christian order of things, and it is sufficient to enable me to illuminate Christianity from this point of view.[51]

CHAPTER EIGHT

The Moment *and the Common Man*

A ll the passages examined in the previous chapters point directly or indirectly toward Kierkegaard's campaign in *The Moment*. In the years just
prior to 1854 it would only have taken a spark to ignite that campaign, but
during those quiet years the spark did not come. Kierkegaard contented
himself that he had said what he wanted to say in *Practice in Christianity*. With
its Introduction and the "Moral" to Part One, *Practice* still occupied a position within the precincts of the established church, albeit dubiously, await-
ing an "admission" from Bishop Mynster. Kierkegaard also had *The Point of
View*, four volumes of his journals and papers, and *Judge for Yourself!* in his
desk drawer. There was nothing in the subsequent *Moment* campaign that
was not said just as trenchantly in these writings. Kierkegaard wanted to
awaken and edify; he wanted to heighten awareness. But people did not
want to hear, and even if they heard, they did not want to act accordingly. For
years Kierkegaard had remained within the precincts of the established order, addressing the clergy — the state church — in vain. From his journals
we can see that it gradually became clear to him that from top to bottom the
clergy was a great *hindrance* in his efforts to awaken and edify the common
man, who constituted his hope for the future of Christianity.

There is an entire literature about Kierkegaard's attack on the church,
one that expresses many varying opinions on the question of whether or
not the attack was a consequence of his previous literary activity. His-
torically, it is a consequence, as Kierkegaard himself believed. If Mynster
had been forthcoming with an admission that his was a watered-down

Christianity concealing the ideal behind his "observations," and had H. L. Martensen not spoken of Mynster as a witness to the truth, Kierkegaard would not have attacked the church — even though, as has been noted, he showed all the elements of an attack in *Practice in Christianity* and in the journals and papers. In that case, even if he had lived a good many years longer and had most likely augmented his canon with several more post-scripts, Kierkegaard would have viewed his work as completed: "For the public, a genius who dies at the age of forty-two never dies at the right time," wrote Georg Brandes in his little book on Kierkegaard, adding: "The mere circumstance that he continued to live would have compelled him to utter radically new and ever truer thoughts."[1] An expression like "radically new and ever truer thoughts" would have amused Kierkegaard. Brandes confronts Kierkegaard with two possibilities: "the leap down into the black abyss of Catholicism or over to the point from which freedom beckons."[2] This would have amused Kierkegaard even more than Brandes's other re-marks; it would have pointed out that even intelligent readers who appreci-ated his work had often failed to realize that this very problem of freedom had been Kierkegaard's fundamental concern in an age of individualism, when freedom had been undermined by a multitude of "freedoms." For his own part, Kierkegaard was thankful to escape from the world, with its joys and torments. In his forty-two years he had accomplished enough to en-sure that the world would not forget him.

But Martensen's rhetorical remarks about Mynster as a witness to the truth struck a nerve in Kierkegaard, coming as they did immediately after a year in which Kierkegaard had occupied himself primarily with this question of the witness to the truth. Now someone has risen to the bait, he thought. The moment had arrived.

The polemical situation in which Kierkegaard placed himself must be evaluated on the basis of his intentions. Kierkegaard's intention was to set forth a corrective, or an ideal, which had to be enunciated in order to mark off the distance between true Christianity, involving contemporaneity and the imitation of Christ, and what Christianity had been transformed into by preaching that took grace in vain. Despite Mynster's death and Martensen's eulogy, Kierkegaard continued to hope that some sort of ad-mission would be forthcoming from the established state church. Specifically, Kierkegaard hoped for an admission from Martensen, which would serve both as a real and as a symbolic acknowledgment that the bishop was able to change his mind and break the silence he had maintained since his initial reply to Kierkegaard's first article. In that reply, Martensen had not shown the slightest understanding of the matter at issue in Kierkegaard's attack. In order to air this question, Kierkegaard had begun his campaign by writing in a newspaper with a large circulation, *Fædrelandet*. This was clearly not easy for him, but his task required it:

> In order to make my contemporaries take notice and in order to deprive the clergy of the excuse that this was something that no one reads, I have used a widely circulated political newspaper.[3]

> This is something I have religiously understood to be my duty, and I thus do it gladly, even though it is personally quite repugnant to me. But humbly before God, and with the dignified self-respect that I dare and ought to have, I will certainly guard against becoming all too familiar with everyone who writes something in a newspaper.[4]

Martensen did in fact reply to Kierkegaard, but in an indirect and teasing fashion, in a sermon he delivered on December 26, 1854, at the consecration of two new bishops in the Church of Our Lady, demonstratively calling upon the new bishops to be "witnesses to the truth"! Now Kierkegaard's patience was *almost* at an end. He bided his time a bit and then continued the attacks in *Fædrelandet*. These attacks included a commentary on the new printing of *Practice in Christianity*. Were that book to be published in its first edition now, Kierkegaard wrote, the Introduction and the "Moral" would be omitted, and the author of the book would no longer be a pseudonym but would be Kierkegaard himself.[5] In its day, *Practice in Christianity* (published 1850) had been Kierkegaard's final attempt to defend the established order. Mynster could have chosen to declare himself either for or against the book, but

> He did neither of the two. He did nothing. He merely wounded himself with the book. And it became clear to me that he was power-

less. Now, on the other hand, I am quite certain about two things, both that, from a Christian point of view, the established order is untenable — that, from a Christian point of view, every day it continues to exist is a crime — *and* that it is impermissible to call upon grace in this manner.[6]

This was Kierkegaard's final appeal to Martensen, but the latter remained silent. Then the decision was made: Kierkegaard dropped Martensen and, with him, the entire cultivated and ecclesiastical world. Now the *moment* and the time of the common man had arrived in earnest. Kierkegaard wrote a farewell article to Martensen in which he asserted that the latter's silence was (1) from a Christian point of view, indefensible, (2) ridiculous, (3) stupidly clever, and (4) contemptible in more than one sense.[7] This article is a bit more heated than the others. For Kierkegaard it was a fateful piece; it was a decisive step away from the church and its clergy and out into the street, to the masses. He had found a passage in Luther in which Luther argued that preaching must not take place in church but in the streets.

Kierkegaard wrote that if he was to be regarded merely as a ranter,

whom the higher clergy did not consider worthy of a reply, then the common man, trusting in the high clergy, might feel justified in concluding that whatever this ranter says (and from a Christian point of view what he says is, in fact, perhaps the most justifiable objection that has ever been raised!) is nonsense. ["Ranter"] is a label that someone in *Dagbladet,* an anonymous writer, probably a spiritual counselor, has already tried to pin on me. He himself was certainly kind enough to grant that I had "great abilities," but he also managed to say that as far as the common man is concerned, what I am saying appears to be "nonsense." Honorable, honest, conscientious spiritual counsel: Say that the common man says so — in order to get him to say it! I, who perhaps actually know the common man, am of another opinion, however. For isn't it so, you common man, that you understand very well — and I think that you in particular can understand this much better and more easily than the demoralized pastors and the corrupted aristocrats — isn't it true that you are very much capable of understanding that it is one thing to be persecuted, mistreated, flogged, crucified, beheaded, and the like, and another thing to be in quite comfortable circumstances, with a family and promotions at regular intervals, all the while earning a living by depicting how someone else was flogged, etc.? But this is also a difference between the Christianity of the New Testament and official Christianity.[8]

With these words Kierkegaard bade farewell to *Fædrelandet* and abandoned his final attempt to initiate a call to arms within the established order of the state church. The only remaining task was to explode the church for the sake of the common man. Kierkegaard now found himself in exactly the same situation as Lindberg in the days of the gatherings out at the limekiln.

Then the first issue of *The Moment* appeared.[9] Despite all his vehemence, in his *Fædrelandet* articles Kierkegaard had held the reins somewhat in check. Now he abandoned all other considerations. A comparison between the *Fædrelandet* articles and *The Moment* will not be undertaken here. The goal of the two stages of Kierkegaard's attack was the same, but in the *Moment* articles the attack took on an earnest pedagogical form and a directness of address that mirrored Kierkegaard's conversations on the street with the common man. Kierkegaard told his reader to take care "not to limit himself to giving an individual issue of *The Moment* a single reading. Since the issue contains a number of articles, on the first reading he should instead acquaint himself with the contents and then later read each article separately."[10] It is exhilarating to read the drafts and commentaries relating to the *Moment* articles in Kierkegaard's papers (volume XI^3). Never before had his prose been so supple and alive, never before had he seemed to have so much spiritual energy, to be as free as he was now, when he could finally speak with all other considerations fallen away. The material had of course been ready for a long time, but this new mode of address, which was appropriate to his new audience, permitted him to take artistic pleasure in serious business.

In the light of this new situation, we should also keep in mind the attack on Grundtvig and his followers that Kierkegaard did not publish.[11]

Of course the Grundtvigians also fought against the state church, against Mynster and Martensen, and high-church elements feared that Kierkegaard and Grundtvig might now form an alliance. Both Kierkegaard and Grundtvig had certainly addressed themselves to the people, the people of the awakenings in Stormgade, the people who had gathered out at the limekiln, at Lyngby Church, and at Frederik's Church, and others as well. Both men had addressed what was called the common man, whether as individuals or as a congregation. But the differences between Kierkegaard and Grundtvig were not clear to everyone. Martensen in particular was nervous about a potential alliance, and he sent his wife and Just Henrik Paulli[12] to listen to Grundtvig preach to his congregation at Vartov to determine whether there was anything in his sermons that could be linked to Kierkegaard's attack on Mynster. Reassured by their report, Martensen wrote to his friend Ludvig Gude,[13] "Yesterday Grundtvig gave an entire sermon against Kierkegaard, whom he assigned to the category 'the mockers say.' . . . I could only delight in learning this, because now the attitude of the entire Grundtvigian movement toward Kierkegaard is clear, and it hadn't been in the beginning."[14]

Kierkegaard's stance in *The Moment* made clear that he had not wanted to get involved with the "awakened" people. In the last chapter I suggested why this was the case, citing a passage from *The Concept of Anxiety* in which Kierkegaard pointed out that "holy" people are characterized by what he called "unfreedom" and "lack of inwardness," i.e., a lack of profound appropriation. Furthermore, the "holy" people thought that as true Christians they ranked higher than others, and Kierkegaard viewed this as an illusion. Here, again, there is a parallel to Lindberg, specifically to Lindberg's attack on the sectarian tendencies of the religious awakenings, the Baptists, and others. But where Kierkegaard took an existential view of the matter, Lindberg had looked at it from the point of view of church politics. Therefore Lindberg had resorted to the Apostles' Creed, to the dissolving of parish boundaries within the People's Church, and, later, to the idea of creating a breathing space through permitting the establishment of elective congregations [*Valgmenigheder*] within the People's Church, as well as the creation of independent congregations. This approach was utterly foreign to Kierkegaard's way of thinking, which here again focused on the individual, specifically on the common man, who had clung to his simplicity and honesty.

In addition to the differences mentioned above, there was yet another decisive dissimilarity between Kierkegaard and Grundtvig, and it had to do with their methods of awakening people. Grundtvig and his followers presented themselves as the true Christians, and the resulting suggestive power of authority either scared people off or attracted them. Kierkegaard, on the other hand, said expressly, "I am not a Christian, but I know what Christianity is," so that people would know he was in the same boat they were in. In this way, Kierkegaard expressed *the idea of solidarity,* by using such phrases as "we are all guilty," "we ordinary people," and "we wretched, miserable common people." Kierkegaard suspected that as soon as Grundtvig had obtained freedom for himself and his followers, he would "permit the continued existence of the entire monstrous illusion, with the state claiming that it is Christian and the people imagining that they are Christian."[15] And if they were granted freedom, Grundtvig and his followers would merely use it to express what they meant by Christianity, namely, "remaining calm and peaceful, reassured in this life, ensconced in their families, and in other respects living as people who are essentially of this world."[16] Thus Grundtvig remained in Vartov, and like his followers he did not "live up to his character" and did not dare to exist in the situation characterized by the "double danger."

At the same time, however, Kierkegaard had to impress indelibly upon the common man that the official representatives of the established order — the pastors and the others authorized by the state — had nothing to do with his awakening. For Kierkegaard, in the wake of Martensen's silence, the official representatives of the state church had nothing to do with the religious life of the common man except as a *hindrance* that had to be pushed aside, so that people could hear the proclamation of true Christianity. And this message came from someone who did not put himself forward as the ideal, who did not claim to be a Christian, who was without authority, and who thus, having expressed his solidarity, wished to direct attention to the corrective — to the ideas of contemporaneity and imitation — that he had proposed. In *The Moment,* Kierkegaard mentioned the book *Practice in Christianity* and its relationship to the established order, saying to the common man: "This [official Christianity's relation to *Practice in Christianity*] is not your affair. On the other hand, if you yourself wish it, the book can help you become aware of this matter of contemporaneity."[17]

Like the rest of his writings, Kierkegaard assigned *The Moment* to the category of "making aware." Kierkegaard did not want to obligate anyone by what he said, and he repeatedly emphasized that he was without authority. He was content to present the ideal and to allow the rest to depend on the free decision of the individual, because "faith is a choice — certainly not a direct reception — and the recipient is the person in whom it becomes apparent whether he will believe or be offended."[18]

Those who know Kierkegaard are aware of the web of reflections that underlay his personal stance during the attack on the church, a stance that was in reality no different from his posture throughout his entire corpus. Only the action, although it remained indirect in form, was different. First, direct action was required in order to abolish the power of the clergy, which constituted the decisive obstacle to reaching the common man. Thereafter, indirect action was needed in order to make the common man aware both of the illusion in which Christendom was living and of what the Christianity of the New Testament demands. In reality, Kierkegaard's most important objective was to stir people to honesty and integrity. He discussed this in the *Fædrelandet* article entitled "What Do I Want?": "Quite simply, I want honesty. . . . I am not Christian strictness as opposed to a supposed Christian leniency. . . . I am neither leniency nor strictness, I am human honesty."[19] Most Kierkegaard scholars have ruminated upon this article without considering the context of action in which it is embedded. For example, in his biography of Kierkegaard,[20] Georg Brandes tore the following sentences from *The Moment* out of context:

> If this, then, is what the generation or the present day wants, if it wants to rebel against Christianity forthrightly, honestly, unreservedly, openly, straightforwardly, and to say to God, "We cannot, we will not submit to this power" — but, mind you, this is to be done forthrightly, honestly, unreservedly, openly, and straightforwardly — well, then, strange as it may seem, I can go along with this, because I want honesty.[21]

Kierkegaard subsequently added,

> For this honesty I will dare. On the other hand, I do not say that it is
> for Christianity that I dare. Suppose this: suppose that I quite liter-
> ally became a sacrifice. I would still not be a sacrifice for Christianity,
> but because I wanted honesty. But even though I dare not say that I
> dare for Christianity, I nonetheless remain fully and blessedly as-
> sured that this daring of mine is pleasing to God, that it has his ap-
> proval.[22]

If in reading this centrally important article in its context one keeps
Kierkegaard's anthropology in mind (and any other reading renders it
meaningless), then it is clear that his real message is this: if Kierkegaard
could awaken the common man to true honesty (which the pastors were
trying to prevent the common man from attaining), then God would certainly see to the rest, in accordance with each individual's capacity, resil-
ience, and strength. At this point we encounter the idea of the "admission"
that opens the way for true grace — grace not used in vain.

From Lindberg's experience, Kierkegaard knew how difficult it was to
conduct such a campaign, which people would much prefer to divert into
the blind alleys of theological debate. This explains Kierkegaard's vehemence, which was certainly not an expression of his mental state. Hans
Brøchner wrote in his memoirs that Kierkegaard had never been as calm,
loving, and even-tempered as during the *Moment* campaign.[23] Kierkegaard's vehemence was appropriate to the matter at hand. He had also
learned something from *The Corsair* about how important it was to interest
the public in a problem, about the importance of "making people aware."
In *On My Work as an Author* he wrote:

> With the direct method, one begins with individuals, a few readers,
> and then the task or the movement is to assemble a mass of people,
> to get hold of an abstraction, the public. In the present case, the *be-
> ginning* was made *maieutically,* starting with something sensational
> and with what accompanies a sensation, the public, which is always
> present when something is brewing. Then the movement was,

119

maieutically, to shake off the "mass" in order to get hold of "the single individual" in the religious sense.[24]

Kierkegaard is here speaking about *Either/Or,* but he employed the very same tactic in his attack on the church, except that in the latter case he found it necessary to exert himself to the utmost with the use of provocative and titillating headlines: "Confirmation and Marriage as Comic Theatre"; "Beware of Those Who Walk in Long Robes"; "What Does the Fire Chief Say?"; "From a Christian Point of View, Christian Child Rearing is Based upon Lies, Sheer Lies"; "The Pastors are Cannibals of the Most Abominable Sort"; "Take an Emetic"; "The State Seduces a Number of Young University Students," and so on.

With this dramatic style, Kierkegaard ensured that his attack would be read in every hole-in-the-wall shop and working-class home in the city. With their exaggerated and aggressive form (not to mention their contents!), the articles unleashed a great many ideas among the sort of people who were generally mute about such matters, and those of the common people who had already been "awakened" found food for thought in them as well. It was frightful! And yet, hadn't there once been someone who had chased the moneychangers out of the forecourts of the temple? And Kierkegaard's biblical passages were right enough. He had turned into a scandal journalist — Martensen was right about that. Kierkegaard himself wrote: "But I am not the least bit afraid of creating a scandal. The Christianity of the New Testament is nothing but sheer scandal, and the word itself is of course the Greek σκάνδαλον *(skandalon),* which the New Testament uses again and again with respect to Christianity."[25] Here Kierkegaard was once again in agreement with Lindberg: no more scratching the surface with polemics — cut to the bone instead. He rebuffed all opponents who came on the scene, referring them to his earlier writings, on which he was now taking a stand. A Dr. Zeuthen stepped forward; he wanted to debate with Kierkegaard and even published a series of writings. But according to Kierkegaard, the people really had no interest in all these dialectics:

> The people have a quite different sort of interest in succinct statements, such as: The public worship of God, as presently constituted,

makes a fool of God. That is something that engages the people. Some think that I am right, others think that I am wrong, but it is something that engages them, while theological erudition, on the other hand, does not. The people, and in particular the common man, are also very capable of understanding the following sort of argument: For a person who, year in and year out, has occupied a royally appointed position with his family and has thus been in the middle of an illusion; for such a person, compared to another person who year after year has made every sacrifice to avoid falling prey to the illusion, and who is now saying that "Christianity is Either/Or"; in comparison to this latter person, for the *former* person to say, "That's the same thing I *said* many years ago": Then the people are very capable of understanding . . . that this is like arguing with an old shoe. I . . . don't really think that Dr. Zeuthen would have come forth with this sort of thing if it weren't for the fact that he — like all of us so-called cultivated people — had been more or less demoralized, Christianly speaking, by Mynster's version of Christianity, while it is possible that the people, on the other hand, have not been demoralized, nor will they be.[26]

In the above-mentioned volume of his papers, which contains extremely pithy and powerful drafts and commentaries related to the articles in *Fædrelandet* and in *The Moment,* Kierkegaard reflected quite deliberately and with great calmness and sobriety upon every step he had taken, including his witty remark that in his sermon in memory of Mynster, Martensen had brought himself "in memory" to the bishop's chair. The remark had amused all of Copenhagen even while it caused offense. Kierkegaard had a hard time escaping the fact that he had made a nasty, witty sort of insinuation, and he spent a couple of pages of rather contorted prose trying to wriggle out of it:

> Thus there is no insinuation whatever on my part here. . . . Just as it is the national bank's concern that all the money it issues, whether pennies or millions, is correctly counted up, so is it very much my concern that nothing that could be called an insinuation issue from

my pen. This is very much my concern, especially right now. Because inasmuch as I am the son (as I remember every day!) of the late Michael Pedersen Kierkegaard, formerly a hosier here in the city (but as is well known, hosiers live in the cellar, indeed, often in the subcellar), I have really felt this, and I will not put up with anything that . . . could prevent me in the least little way from fully feeling my dignity when confronted with the low insinuations of a velvet bishop.[27]

This volume of Kierkegaard's papers also contains a very beautiful sketch of Mynster as a person: Mynster himself surely would have refused to be labeled a witness to the truth, etc. But Kierkegaard also made the firm assertion that *"from a Christian point of view,* Mynster's version of Christianity was watered down in two senses of the term: it was a pale variant, lacking in character; and no matter how well-intended, if the New Testament is to be judge of what Christianity is, Mynster's version is a hallucination."[28]

The same volume holds Kierkegaard's final memorial to his father. In his reply to Kierkegaard's piece on Mynster, Martensen had insinuated that Kierkegaard had abandoned his obligation of piety toward his father.

This is a shameless untruth. I have said that it had been my life's misfortune that — partly out of piety toward my deceased father, who had brought me up with Mynster's sermons — I had accepted at face value the notion that Mynster was a man of character instead of protesting against it. What shamelessness to want to use this to demonstrate that I have emancipated myself from a relationship of piety toward my late father. . . . In actuality I have not only spoken of the work of love of remembering someone deceased[29] (him, my late father), I have also put it into practice. Almost all of my life has been dedicated to being his son, to remembering him. Not a day has passed when I have not remembered him. I have remembered him today as well, as I will also do tomorrow and so on until the end. Yes, I have remembered him, and it was also out of piety toward him that

I endured everything in my relationship with Bishop Mynster as long as Mynster lived. And the truth, which surely will see the light of day at some point, is that Bishop Mynster abused my melancholia and took advantage of the fact that, owing to this relationship to my father, I was willing to put up with just about anything.[30]

I will not endeavor to sort out the assumptions made and the various positions taken in the continuing debate about Kierkegaard's *Moment* campaign. My few forays into this complicated situation are undertaken only with respect to the question of the common man, and they conclude with *the* common man behind the whole affair, Kierkegaard's father.

After Martensen's dogged silence, Kierkegaard abandoned *Fædrelandet*. He dropped the established order, with its cultivation and its ecclesiastical retinue, and took to the streets with *The Moment,* pinning all his hopes for the future of Christianity upon the awakening of the common man, whom he wanted to help first out of the deceptions of the pastors and thereafter into an environment of sincerity and honesty — and God would surely see to the rest. Kierkegaard was able to maintain a faint hope for the pastors *if* they would incorporate his corrective message into their preaching of Christianity, thus compelling people to confront the "admission" that alone gives meaning to grace.

This is the line of thinking Kierkegaard adopted in a piece called "Looking at Stars," which was not included in *The Moment.* Here Kierkegaard referred to an old Christmas game, in which a player paid off a forfeit by entering a darkened room and "looking at stars." Kierkegaard had several people at the party go into the room one after the other, but in each case the person was not alone. God was also present and said to each, "Are you a Christian?" Each person answered after his or her own fashion. A pastor also went in: "Now have him forget everything. . . . Have him think only of one thing with all his passion, namely that God is present and is asking him, 'Are you a Christian? As a teacher you have bound yourself with a sacred vow. . . . Therefore, if you are not a Christian you have a great deal to answer for. Nevertheless that should not decide the question, no. But your honesty should.'"[31] The pastor then had to admit that he is no Christian, and he said,

"But now that I have had this insight into myself and have made this confession to you, I assume it is necessary, then, that I give up my position [as a pastor]." "No, my friend, no. Just remain in your position, but do not forget to drill into [*indøve*] your congregation that this, after all, is not really Christianity. If you do this, and if you do your job in other respects, I will give you my blessing so that someday, when you die, you will be able to find happiness in the fact that your life has really been beneficial. There is only one thing you must not do, not for anything, or I will allow this great responsibility, which is hanging over your head by a single horsehair, to come crushing down upon you with the force of more than a hundredweight. You must not pretend to be clever; you must not be a diplomat and make crafty maneuvers, saying, 'We must conceal this from the congregation.' This alone, you must not do."[32]

Here we see Kierkegaard grappling with the idea of the "admission" that he had demanded of the clergy of his times as a condition of their remaining within the boundaries of the established order, the state church. He did add, however, that this piece dates from before the end of 1854.[33] Once again Kierkegaard stressed honesty as the decisive factor, and in this way he connected this older piece with the article in *Fædrelandet* in which he insisted that he wanted honesty. Simply to arrive at an honest posture is enough. This in turn is connected to Kierkegaard's insistence that where Christianity is concerned, it is the *how* and not the *what* that matters. But Kierkegaard was a thinker, and thus he also had a reply for the many who anxiously inquired about doctrine — the *what* of Christianity. Kierkegaard based his writing on his anthropology (man as a synthesis of the temporal and the eternal), which one must always bear in mind when examining his categories, and he referred to a passage in the *Postscript*[34] in which Johannes Climacus shows that, "remarkably enough, there is a *how* with the characteristic that, when it is indicated exactly, also indicates a *what*. . . . This is the how of *faith*. So here, right at its very maximum, inwardness is again shown to be objectivity."[35] This is an important instance of Kierkegaard's use of his idea of subjectivity in connection with Christianity, and here we see the link between subjectivity and the category of honesty, which in turn formed the foundation of the entire *Moment* campaign. Naturally, one does not become a Christian simply by being honest, but in Christendom the category of honesty is the same for the wise and the simple. Honesty is the necessary precondition for God to have anything to do with a person, and at the same time this very honesty forbids concealing the absolute requirement found in the New Testament. It is by means of this category of honesty that Kierkegaard sought to carry out his task of introducing Christianity into Christendom, which of course already possessed the doctrine.

But no admission was forthcoming, neither after the indirect appeal in *Practice in Christianity* nor after Mynster's death, when Kierkegaard made a direct appeal in *Fædrelandet.* On the contrary, Martensen and the clergy had hardened their stance, so the clergy was the illusion that had to be shoved aside. This was the theme of all ten issues of *The Moment.* As we have seen, because of the exigencies of the situation, Kierkegaard quite deliberately became a quarrelsome person and a scandal-mongering journalist in middle-class Copenhagen.

A month before he collapsed unconscious on the street and was taken to Frederik's Hospital to die, Kierkegaard wrote the last article of his life, dated September 1, 1855, and intended for the next issue of *The Moment.* He felt that death was not far off and entitled the article "My Task." In addition to some reflections on the struggle in which Kierkegaard was then engaged, the article contains a combined homage and appeal to the two courts of judgment to which, whenever there had been questions concerning his goals or methods, he had always turned throughout his writing career, and especially at this time: *Socrates* and *the common man.* Kierkegaard had begun his writing career with his dissertation on Socrates. Now, in the shadows of evening, with death approaching, Kierkegaard recalled Socrates once again:

> You, noble, simple man of antiquity: you are the only *human being* I acknowledge with admiration as a thinker. Very little has been preserved about you, who of all human beings are the only true martyr to intellect, equally great as a person of character and as a thinker. But how infinitely much this little is! Oh, how I long for a mere half hour's conversation with you, far away from these battalions of

thinkers that "Christendom" puts into the field under the name "Christian thinkers"![36]

Kierkegaard recalled Socrates' situation and his battle against the Sophists as well as his own situation, in which he did battle against the Sophists of his era, the pastors. Socrates did not claim that he was knowledgeable, but insisted that he was ignorant, just as Kierkegaard did not call himself a Christian. But this was exactly why people could not dismiss them, because they knew that, in Socrates' case, everyone else was just as ignorant as Socrates, and in Kierkegaard's case, everyone else was just as little a Christian as Kierkegaard:

> But, just as . . . you made many enemies by making it clear that they were ignorant; and just as they imputed to you the inference that you yourself must be what you could demonstrate that the others were not (and for that they bore an envious grudge against you) — all this has been my lot as well. It has provoked bitter feelings against me because I can make it plain that other people are even less Christian than I am, who at least have enough of a relation to Christianity that I truly see and acknowledge the fact that I am not a Christian.[37]

No, no one can claim to be a Christian. The only salvation is, first of all, honesty and the admission that one is humbled, crushed under the weight of this high ideal. Thereafter, the only things remaining are grace and God's mercy. This was what Kierkegaard said to the religion of his times. He believed that he had been brought up in order to be sacrificed for the sake of this challenge to Christendom:

> And the infinite grace that has been and still is being shown me is to be chosen to be a sacrifice, to be chosen for this, yes, and then one more thing: under the combined influence of the Almighty and of Love, to have been developed to the point at which I could maintain that this [being a sacrifice] is the highest degree of grace that the God of Love can demonstrate toward anyone.[38]

Kierkegaard concluded this final article with these words:

You common man! The Christianity of the New Testament is something infinitely high, but of course it is not high in a manner that has to do with the differences between one person and another with respect to talent and the like. No, it is for everyone. . . .

You common man! I have not cut off my life from yours. You know it; I have lived in the streets and am known by everyone. Moreover, I have never amounted to anything and am possessed of no class egotism. So if I belong to anyone, I must belong to you, you common man; you, although you once were misled by someone who made money off you by pretending to promote your interests; you, who were willing enough to find me and my existence ludicrous; you, who nonetheless have less reason than anyone to be impatient or unappreciative of the fact that I am with you — something the more aristocratic people have had greater reason to be, seeing as I have not given them my decisive support and have maintained only a loose connection with them.

You common man! I make no secret that, according to my notions, being a Christian is something so infinitely high that there are always only a few individuals who attain it. (This is confirmed both by Christ's life, when you examine it in the context of his times, and by the implications of his preaching, when you take it seriously.) Nonetheless it is possible for anyone. But for the sake of God in Heaven and by everything that is holy, there is one thing I implore you to do: avoid the pastors, avoid them, these abominable people whose way of making a living is to prevent you from even becoming aware of what true Christianity is. . . . Avoid them, but take care that you willingly and promptly pay them the money they require. . . . Pay them double, so that your disagreement with them becomes entirely clear, namely that what concerns them, money, does not concern you in the least, and that, on the other hand, what does not concern them concerns you infinitely — Christianity.[39]

These were Kierkegaard's last words to his Danish contemporaries, who had wanted to shake him off so that they could peacefully busy themselves with their cultural pastimes, all the while providing themselves with a sort of religious alibi. As mentioned above, a month after writing this article, Kierkegaard collapsed, unconscious, on his battleground, the street. He was taken to Frederik's Hospital and died there on November 11, 1855, pleased with his accomplishments and thankful to God, who had helped him. In his final diary entry, dated September 25, 1855, speaking of himself in the third person, Kierkegaard put forth his fundamental philosophical position one last time. God had helped him

> to the extent that God can help attain what in fact can only be accomplished by freedom. Only freedom can do it. But what is surprising is to be able to express oneself by thanking God for it, as if it were God who did it. And in his joy at being able to do this. . . . he is so happy that he will hear nothing, nothing, about his having done it himself, but he thankfully refers everything to God and prays God that it might remain so, that it is God who does it — because he does not have faith in himself, but he does have faith in God.[40]

After having publicly taken leave of the common man, with these words Kierkegaard personally took leave of the world, which had been both a hall of delights and a vale of tears.

What remained was a matter of little importance in the present context, the burial. As a quarrelsome person and a scandal-mongering journalist Kierkegaard had insured that his funeral would not take place with timpani and trumpets, with the church choir packed with clergy in their finest vestments, and the rest of the church brimming with the stars and stalwarts of the cultural firmament. None of them showed up. But it was nonetheless a proper funeral, between two Sunday services at the Church of Our Lady, where Kierkegaard had so often heard Mynster and just as often had met Regine, who only a few months earlier had traveled all the way to the West Indies but had managed to say goodbye to him first. That one time Regine had dared to confront him directly, saying, "God bless you. May all go well with you, and goodbye."[41] (The memory of this last meeting had been a source of joy to Kierkegaard on his deathbed.) His brother gave him a proper eulogy. Archdeacon Eggert Christopher Tryde[42] was obligated by his position to officiate at the burial, and naturally some family members were also there. His niece Henriette Lund sat up in the church gallery and became quite worried because the church was full of a large number of sinister-looking people of the simple class, who crowded around the little coffin in the nave of the church. Fortunately, she wrote in her memoirs, a number of university students forced their way through the crowd and took up positions around the coffin.[43]

From his window in the bishop's palace opposite the church, Martensen followed what he could see of the event. That same evening, November 18, 1855, he wrote to his friend Ludvig Gude:

> Today, after a service at the Church of Our Lady, Kierkegaard was buried; there was a large cortège of mourners (in grand style, how ironic!). We have scarcely seen the equal of the *tactlessness* shown by the family in having him buried on a *Sunday,* between two religious services, from the nation's *most important* church. It could not be prevented by law, however, although it could have been prevented by *proper* conduct, which Tryde lacked here as he does everywhere it is required. Kierkegaard's brother spoke at the church (as a brother, not as a pastor). At this point I do not know anything at all about what he said and how he said it. The newspapers will soon be running a spate of these burial stories. I understand the cortège was primarily composed of young people and a large number of obscure personages. There were no dignitaries, unless one wishes to include R. Nielsen[44] and Magister Stilling[45] in this category.[46]

This was the final salutation Kierkegaard received from the cultivated class, but the poor and simple people escorted the coffin out to Assistens Cemetery, where he was buried next to his father, mother, and deceased siblings. There was no memorial plaque for him, nor was his name inscribed with the others on the little sandstone tablet at the grave. There is a series of letters about this matter from his brother, who became Bishop of Aalborg. The nieces and nephews were pressing him about the grave, and finally letters concerning the matter began to arrive from abroad. But Peter Christian Kierkegaard, who was now old and had become even more pusillanimous (as Søren Kierkegaard had called him) than ever, could not really make up his mind. Perhaps (Peter Christian hinted at something along these lines) his hesitation was based on the profound and accurate idea that what would suit his brother best would be *not* to have such an earthly monument. In life, when his innermost thoughts were concerned, Søren had worked indirectly and in concealment. Now he was concealed by the earth, freed from that body of mortality that had caused him such pain in life.

But Søren Kierkegaard himself had considered this matter in his journals, and it had seemed to him that after all a little visible reminder of where he was buried might well be in order. Finally, in 1875, twenty years after his death, he received his memorial plaque at the family gravesite. Inscribed on it was the verse by Brorson[47] he had wanted:

In a little while,
I shall have won,
Then the entire battle
Will disappear at once.
Then I may rest
In halls of roses
And unceasingly
And unceasingly
Speak with my Jesus.[48]

A Brief Guide to Søren Kierkegaard's Writings in English Translation

The standard English language edition of Kierkegaard's complete published works (plus a number of things he did not publish) is *Kierkegaard's Writings,* ed. Howard V. Hong and Edna H. Hong, 26 vols. (Princeton, NJ: Princeton University Press, 1978-2000), which is available by individual volumes as well as by complete set. Several of Kierkegaard's works are also available in other editions, most notably Alastair Hannay's excellent translations of *Either/Or, Fear and Trembling,* and *The Sickness Unto Death,* available in Penguin editions. Below is a list of Kierkegaard's published works with titles translated as they appear in the Princeton edition of *Kierkegaard's Writings* and listed in the order in which they appear in that edition.

Early Polemical Writings [including newspaper articles from Kierkegaard's student days, *From the Papers of One Still Living,* and the unpublished piece *The Battle Between the Old and the New Soap-Cellars*] (vol. I)

The Concept of Irony [also includes Kierkegaard's unpublished notes from Schelling's lectures in Berlin, 1841-42] (vol. II)

Either/Or, parts I and II (vols. III and IV)

Eighteen Upbuilding Discourses (vol. V)

Fear and Trembling and *Repetition* (vol. VI)

Philosophical Fragments [also includes the unpublished manuscript *Johannes Climacus, or De omnibus dubitandum est*] (vol. VII)

The Concept of Anxiety (vol. VIII)

Prefaces [also includes the unpublished manuscript *Writing Sampler*] (vol. IX)

Three Discourses on Imagined Occasions (vol. X)

Stages on Life's Way (vol. XI)

Concluding Unscientific Postscript (vol. XII.1 and XII.2)

The Corsair Affair [not a published work *per se,* but a series of documents related to Kierkegaard's collision with *The Corsair* as well as a number of Kierkegaard's other articles related to his writings] (vol. XIII)

Two Ages [properly entitled *A Literary Review,* this is Kierkegaard's book-length review of a novel entitled *Two Ages*] (vol. XIV)

Upbuilding Discourses in Various Spirits (vol. XV)

Works of Love (vol. XVI)

Christian Discourses and *The Crisis and a Crisis in the Life of an Actress* (vol. XVII)

Without Authority [the translators' collective title for the following works: *The Lily of the Field and the Bird of the Air, Two Ethical-Religious Essays, Three Discourses at the Communion on Fridays, An Upbuilding Discourse,* and *Two Discourses at the Communion on Fridays*] (vol. XVIII)

The Sickness Unto Death (vol. XIX)

Practice in Christianity (vol. XX)

For Self-Examination and *Judge for Yourself!* [the latter work not published by Kierkegaard] (vol. XXI)

The Point of View [the translators' collective title for the following works: *On My Work as an Author, The Point of View for My Work as an Author,* and *Armed Neutrality* (the latter two works not published by Kierkegaard)] (vol. XXII)

The Moment and Late Writings [the translators' collective title for the following works: articles from *Fædrelandet,* 1854-55; *The Moment; This Must Be Said, So Let It Be Said; Christ's Judgment on Official Christianity;* and *The Changelessness of God*] (vol. XXIII)

The Book on Adler [not published by Kierkegaard] (vol. XXIV)

Letters and Documents (vol. XXV)

Cumulative Index (vol. XXVI)

The most comprehensive English language edition of Kierkegaard's unpublished writings is *Søren Kierkegaard's Journals and Papers,* ed. and trans.

Howard V. Hong and Edna H. Hong, 7 vols. (Bloomington, IN, and London: Indiana University Press, 1967-1978). This edition, while large in scope, has the drawback that four of its six volumes of text (the seventh volume is an index volume) are organized alphabetically by topics, as determined by the editors and translators, an arrangement which inevitably introduces an element of arbitrariness and which makes it difficult to observe the development of Kierkegaard's thought over time. Thus, although this edition is still "standard" in one sense, most readers might well profit more from Alastair Hannay's excellent translation of Søren Kierkegaard, *Papers and Journals: A Selection* (London and New York: Penguin, 1996).

Endnotes

Note to the Introduction

1. In Kierkegaard's Danish of the 1840s, as in Jørgen Bukdahl's Danish of the 1950s, the phrase "common man" had none of the invidious overtones that have been attributed to it more recently.

Notes to Chapter One

1. Poul Martin Møller (1794-1838), philosopher and author, taught at the University of Copenhagen, where he was Kierkegaard's mentor and favorite professor.

2. Frederik Christian Sibbern (1785-1872), professor of philosophy, wrote works on ethics, psychology, metaphysics, politics, and religion; he was Kierkegaard's professor and friend.

3. Adam Oehlenschlæger (1779-1850), Danish poet and playwright, introduced romantic poetry into Denmark; his reputation was established with collections of his poems published in 1802 and 1805.

4. Hans Christian Ørsted (1777-1851) was the most famous Danish scientist of the age; he discovered electromagnetism.

5. Hans Lassen Martensen (1808-84), theologian, professor at the University of Copenhagen, and subsequently Bishop of Zealand, served as Kierkegaard's tutor during the latter's years as a university student. Martensen's principal contribution to speculative theology was *Den christelige Dogmatik* [Christian Dogmatics] (Copenhagen: C. A. Reitzel, 1849).

6. N. F. S. Grundtvig (1783-1872) was a pastor, poet, theologian, and spokes-man for both religious and national "awakening."

7. *Søren Kierkegaards Samlede Værker* [The Collected Works of Søren Kierke-gaard], ed. A. B. Drachmann, J. L. Heiberg, and H. O. Lange, 1st ed., 14 vols. (Co-penhagen: Gyldendal, 1901-6), vol. VII, p. 70 (hereafter *SV*).

In the notes to the present volume, although all translations from Kierke-gaard's works have been made by the translator, reference will also be given in square brackets to the standard English language translation of Kierkegaard's com-plete works: *Kierkegaard's Writings,* ed. Howard V. Hong and Edna H. Hong, 26 vols. (Princeton, NJ: Princeton University Press, 1978-2000) (hereafter *"KW"* fol-lowed by volume number, page number, and in parentheses the English language title of the specific work being cited), vol. XII.1, p. 89 *(Concluding Unscientific Post-script)*. The complete version of this note is thus: *SV* VII, p. 70 [*KW* XII.1, p. 89 *(Concluding Unscientific Postscript)*].

8. Cf. *SV* VII, p. 295 [*KW* XII.1, pp. 340-41 *(Concluding Unscientific Postscript)*], and IX, p. 363 [*KW* XVI, pp. 383-84 *(Works of Love)*].

9. One of the basic axioms of traditional Aristotelian logic is the principle of contradiction, that is, that "A" is not "not-A."

Notes to Chapter Two

1. Henrich Steffens (1773-1845), Norwegian-Danish philosopher, was ini-tially influenced by Romanticism but became more conservative and orthodox in his views as time went by. Steffens spent most of his career in Germany.

2. Henrich Steffens, *Indledning til philosophiske Forelæsninger* [Introduction to Philosophical Lectures], ed. Johnny Kondrup (Copenhagen: C. A. Reitzel, 1996), pp. 18-19.

3. Steffens, *Indledning,* pp. 18-19.

4. Cf. *SV* XIII, pp. 184-97, esp. p. 192 [*KW* II, pp. 95-111, esp. pp. 103-5 *(The Concept of Irony)*].

5. Cf. *Søren Kierkegaards Papirer* [The Papers of Søren Kierkegaard], ed. P. A. Heiberg, V. Kuhr, and E. Torsting, 2nd enlarged edition by N. Thulstrup, index by N. J. Cappelørn, 16 vols. in 25 tomes (Copenhagen: Gyldendal, 1968-78), I A 250, 251, 260, and 263. References will be in the following form: *"Pap.";* followed by volume number; followed by a superscript tome number for volumes that have been divided into tomes; followed by "A" (the letter assigned by the editors to ordi-nary journal entries), "B" (the letter assigned by the editors to drafts of material

subsequently published or intended for publication), or "C" (the letter assigned to reading notes and similar material); followed by the serial number assigned by the editors to entries grouped under that volume, tome, and letter designation (followed by a page number when necessary). The format of the present note is typical: *Pap.* I A 250, 251, 260, and 263.

In the notes to the present volume, although all translations from Kierkegaard's journals and papers have been made by the translator, reference will also be given to the most comprehensive English language translation of Kierkegaard's journals and papers: *Søren Kierkegaard's Journals and Papers,* ed. and trans. Howard V. Hong and Edna H. Hong, 7 vols. (Bloomington, IN, and London: Indiana University Press, 1967-78) (hereafter *"SKJP"* followed by the serial number assigned by the Hong edition to the passage in question). Where, as in most cases, a citation from Kierkegaard's journals and papers appears in translation in the Hong edition, reference to the Hong translation will appear in square brackets following the reference to the Danish edition. The complete version of the present note is thus: *Pap.* I A 250 [*SKJP* 2304], 251 [*SKJP* 2305], 260, and 263.

6. *Pap.* I A 264 [*SKJP* 1629].

7. *Pap.* I C 46 [*SKJP* 5077], 47 [*SKJP* 5078], 48 [*SKJP* 5079], 49 [*SKJP* 5080], 50 [*SKJP* 1186], 51 [*SKJP* 5083], 52 [*SKJP* 5084], 53 [*SKJP* 5085], 54 [*SKJP* 5086], 55, 56 [*SKJP* 3845], 57, 58 [*SKJP* 1179], 59, 60 [*SKJP* 5109], 61 [*SKJP* 5110], 62 [*SKJP* 5111], 63, 64 [*SKJP* 5112], 65 [*SKJP* 5087], 66 [*SKJP* 2206], 67, 68, 69 [*SKJP* 3846], 70 [*SKJP* 3847], 71, 72 [*SKJP* 5120], 73 [*SKJP* 1455], 74 [*SKJP* 5121], 75 [*SKJP* 5122], 76 [*SKJP* 5123], 77 [*SKJP* 5124], 78 [SKJP 5125], 79 [*SKJP* 5126], 80 [*SKJP* 831], 81 [*SKJP* 5127], 82 [*SKJP* 5128], 83 [*SKJP* 5129], 84 [*SKJP* 5130], 85 [*SKJP* 5131], 86, 87 [*SKJP* 5134], 88 [*SKJP* 5135], 89 [*SKJP* 5137], 90, 91, 92, 93, 94, 95 [*SKJP* 5138], 96 [*SKJP* 5139], 97, 98, 99, 100 [*SKJP* 5158], 101 [*SKJP* 5159], 102 [*SKJP* 5160], 103 [*SKJP* 5163], 104 [*SKJP* 5165], 105 [*SKJP* 5166], 106 [*SKJP* 5167], 107 [*SKJP* 5168], 108 [*SKJP* 5169], 109 [*SKJP* 5170], 110 [*SKJP* 5171], 111 [*SKJP* 5172], 112 [*SKJP* 5173], 113 [*SKJP* 2703], 114, 115, 116 [*SKJP* 5193], 117 [*SKJP* 5194], 118 [*SKJP* 5195], 119 [*SKJP* 5196], 120 [*SKJP* 5197], 121 [*SKJP* 5198], 122, 123 [*SKJP* 5199], 124 [*SKJP* 5192], 125 *SKJP* 4397], 126 [*SKJP* 4398], 127.

8. *Pap.* I C 102, pp. 275-76 [*SKJP* 5160].

9. *SV* I, p. 72 [*KW* III, p. 91 (*Either/Or,* part one)].

10. Peter Wilhelm (or Vilhelm) Lund (1801-80) was a brother of two of Søren Kierkegaard's brothers-in-law and a well-known and widely respected natural scientist; he traveled to Brazil in 1832 and remained there for most of his adult life.

11. Peter Engel Lind (1814-1903) was a pastor and theologian who matricu-

lated into the University of Copenhagen in 1831 and was one of Kierkegaard's friends at the university.

12. *Breve og Aktstykker vedrørende Søren Kierkegaard* [Letters and Documents Concerning Søren Kierkegaard], ed. Niels Thulstrup, 2 vols. (Copenhagen: Munksgaard, 1953-54), vol. I, pp. 33-35 (hereafter *B&A*) [*KW* XXV, pp. 41-47 *(Letters and Documents)*].

13. *B&A* I, p. 38 [*KW* XXV, pp. 48-49 *(Letters and Documents)*].

14. Friedrich Wilhelm Schelling (1775-1854) was a German idealist philosopher known for his opposition to Hegel. Kierkegaard attended Schelling's lectures in Berlin during the winter of 1841-42, but was not impressed.

15. During Napoleon's occupation of Germany, Friedrich Ludwig Jahn (1778-1852) sought to restore the morale of German youth by starting a movement that emphasized physical fitness and gymnastics; for several years Jahn's movement was wildly popular.

16. *SV* XIII, p. 192 [*KW* II, p. 104 *(The Concept of Irony)*].

17. Peter Johannes Spang (1796-1846) was the pastor at the Church of the Holy Spirit in Copenhagen and one of Kierkegaard's companions on his daily walks.

18. *B&A* I, p. 77 [*KW* XXV, p. 97 *(Letters and Documents)*].

19. *B&A* I, pp. 83-84 [*KW* XXV, pp. 106-7 *(Letters and Documents)*].

20. *Breve til og fra F. C. Sibbern* [Letters to and from F. C. Sibbern], ed. C. L. N. Mynster, vol. II (Copenhagen: Gyldendal, 1868), p. 76.

21. *Breve til og fra F. C. Sibbern*, p. 82.

22. See Henrich Steffens, *Christliche Religionsphilosophie,* Part I, *Theologie* (Breslau: Josef Max, 1839), pp. 440ff. (based on Kierkegaard's reference).

23. *Pap.* VIII^1 A 331 [*SKJP* 3049].

24. Steffens, *Christliche Religionsphilosophie,* Part II, *Ethik,* p. 260 (based on Kierkegaard's reference).

25. Steffens, *Christliche Religionsphilosophie,* Part II, *Ethik,* p. 262 (based on Kierkegaard's reference). The cited passage from Kierkegaard's papers is from *Pap.* VIII^1 A 337.

26. *Pap.* IX A 141 [*SKJP* 2641]; this passage is followed by Kierkegaard's marginal note: "There are some remarks in this connection somewhere in H. Steffens' *Anthropologie.*"

27. *Pap.* V B 53, p. 18 [*KW* VIII, p. 187 *(The Concept of Anxiety)*].

28. Torsten Bohlin, *Kierkegaards dogmatiska Åskådning* [Kierkegaard's View of Dogmatics] (Stockholm: Diakonistyrelsen, 1925), pp. 155-57.

29. *SV* IV, p. 330n [*KW* VIII, p. 59n *(The Concept of Anxiety)*].

30. Grundtvig's *Kirkens Gienmæle* [The Church's Reply] was a slashing attack on the moderately rationalistic theology of H. N. Clausen, a professor of New Testament at the University of Copenhagen. In response to the attack, Clausen brought a successful libel suit against Grundtvig, which proved to be a turning point in the latter's career.

31. Kristian Kold (1816-70) was one of the founders of the folk high school movement for popular enlightenment.

Notes to Chapter Three

1. Jacob Christian Lindberg (1797-1857) was a renowned scholar of Hebrew, respected Bible-translator, sharp-witted and charismatic controversialist on the "anti-rationalist" side in theological matters, occasional ally of Grundtvig, and pastor.

2. Nytorv [literally, "New Market"] is a large square in the center of Copenhagen.

3. *Pap.* I C 2 [*SKJP* 5053].

4. Jakob Peter Mynster (1775-1854) was Bishop of Zealand and Primate of Denmark from 1834 until his death. He was the most important representative of the established church, particularly popular among the upper and upper-middle classes in Copenhagen, and on relatively close terms with the Kierkegaard family. Initially, Søren Kierkegaard had the highest respect for him.

5. *SV* VII, pp. 30n, 34 [*KW* XII.1, pp. 41n, 46 *(Concluding Unscientific Postscript)*].

6. Hans Christian Andersen (1805-75) was a poet, novelist, and writer of fairy tales; he was the target of criticism in Kierkegaard's first book, *From the Papers of One Still Living*.

7. Peter Christian Kierkegaard (1805-88) was Søren Kierkegaard's elder brother; he was a theologian, a follower of Grundtvig, a pastor in the Danish Church, Bishop of Aalborg (1856-75), and briefly a cabinet minister (1867-68).

8. The title of Grundtvig's work *Braga Talk* has become a Danish pejorative term for the high-flown rhetoric and Norse-style jargon typical of Grundtvig and his school.

9. *Pap.* I A 60 [*SKJP* 5089].

10. N. F. S. Grundtvig, *Om den sande Christendom,* first published January-June 1826 in *Theologisk Maanedskrift* and subsequently in *Nik. Fred. Sev. Grundtvigs ud-*

valgte Skrifter [Selected Writings of Nik. Fred. Sev. Grundtvig], ed. Holger Begtrup, vol. IV (Copenhagen: Gyldendal, 1906), p. 505.

11. *Pap* VII^2 B 235, p. 200 [*KW* XXIV, p. 113 *(The Book on Adler)*].

12. Cf. *SV* VIII, pp. 1-105, especially p. 59 [*KW* XIV, pp. 1-112, esp. pp. 62-63 *(Two Ages)*].

13. *Pap.* V B 150, 27 [*KW* XI, p. 646 *(Stages on Life's Way)*].

Notes to Chapter Four

1. Michael Pedersen Kierkegaard (1756-1838) started out as a poor shepherd boy on the heaths of West Jutland, went to Copenhagen at the age of 11 or 12, apprenticed himself to an uncle who dealt in dry goods, soon became an independent businessman, and eventually was quite well-to-do. He was able to retire at the age of forty and support a large household quite comfortably on the income from his investments. In 1797 he married his distant cousin and housekeeper, Ane Sørensdatter Lund, by whom he had seven children, of whom the youngest was Søren Aabye Kierkegaard.

2. *Pap.* XI^2 A 419.

3. *Intelligensblade,* no. 41-42 (January 1, 1844), Bd. 4, pp. 97ff.; cf. esp. p. 101.

4. Georg Brandes, *Søren Kierkegaard. En kritisk Fremstilling i Grundrids* [Søren Kierkegaard: Outlines of a Critical Exposition], in *Samlede Skrifter* [Collected Writings], 2nd ed., *Danmark,* vol. II (Copenhagen: Gyldendal, 1919), pp. 240-41. Georg Brandes (1842-1927) was a modernist critic and freethinker who appreciated and was influenced by Kierkegaard, whom he attempted to interpret in such a way as to support his own atheistic views. See Chapter Eight for further discussion of Brandes's attempt to interpret Kierkegaard for his own ends.

5. Stormgade is a street not far (200-300 yards) from the Kierkegaard family home. The site where the meeting hall of the Moravian congregation once stood is now occupied by a part of the Danish National Museum.

6. Hans Brøchner (1820-75) was a philosopher and professor at the University of Copenhagen. His recollections of Kierkegaard, to whom he was distantly related, were published posthumously. See Bruce H. Kirmmse, *Encounters with Kierkegaard* (Princeton, NJ: Princeton University Press, 1996), pp. 225-52 for Brøchner's recollections of Kierkegaard.

7. Frederik Hammerich (1809-77) was a church historian and professor, as well as a follower of Grundtvig and friend of Peter Christian Kierkegaard.

8. Regine Schlegel, née Olsen (1822-1904), was Kierkegaard's fiancée from

September 1840 until October 1841. She later married [Johan] Frederik ("Fritz") Schlegel (1817-96).

9. Carl Joachim Brandt (1817-89) was a pastor and historian of Danish literature. He was an important supporter of Grundtvig.

10. Emil Boesen (1812-79) was a pastor in Jutland and subsequently archdeacon in Aarhus. He was a schoolmate, close confidant, and lifelong friend of Kierkegaard.

11. Author's note: I have written elsewhere of Michael Pedersen Kierkegaard and the religious life of his native district in *Søren Kierkegaard, hans fader og slægten i Sædding* [Søren Kierkegaard, His Father, and the Family in Sædding] (Ribe: Dansk Hjemstavnsforlag, 1960).

12. *Pap.* X³ A 338 [*SKJP* 1874].

13. Peter Larsen Skræppenborg (1802-73) was a leader in the religious awakening movement.

14. Bethesda Church is the Copenhagen headquarters of the Inner Mission movement. Vartov was a home for elderly women where Grundtvig was granted a parish in 1839; it quickly became the center for the Grundtvigian movement and remains so to this day.

15. The phrase cited in the text is taken from Kierkegaard's conversations in the hospital with his friend Emil Boesen, published in *Af Søren Kierkegaards efterladte Papirer. 1854-55* [From the Posthumous Papers of Søren Kierkegaard, 1854-55], ed. H. Gottsched (Copenhagen: C. A. Reitzel, 1881), p. 596. An English translation of these conversations is available in Kirmmse, *Encounters with Kierkegaard,* pp. 121-28; see p. 125.

16. Bone Falch Rønne (1764-1833) was a pastor, popular evangelist, and religious pamphleteer.

17. Cited from the paraphrase by Kaj Baagø, *Magister Jacob Christian Lindberg* (Copenhagen: Gad, 1958), p. 112.

18. "Professors" is crossed out [in Lindberg's original manuscript]. [Note in Baagø, *Magister Jacob Christian Lindberg,* p. 112.]

19. The cited passage, which is partly Baagø's paraphrase and partly Baagø's direct citation from the original source, is here cited from Baagø, *Magister Jacob Christian Lindberg,* p. 113.

20. Christen Madsen (1776-1829) was a leader of the first generation of the religious awakening movement. Rasmus Sørensen (1799-1865), Rasmus Ottesen (1803-62), and Jens Jørgensen (1806-86) were active in the second generation of the religious awakening movement and went on to become political spokesmen

for the peasant cause. For Peter Larsen Skræppenborg and for Kristian Kold, see note 13 in this chapter and Chapter Two, note 31, respectively.

21. N. F. S. Grundtvig, "Til min egen Meta" [To My Own Meta], from July 1845, but first published posthumously in 1885 and subsequently in *Nik. Fred. Sev. Grundtvigs udvalgte Skrifter,* vol. IX (Copenhagen: Gyldendal, 1909), p. 42.

22. Henrik Nicolai Clausen (1793-1877) was a moderate rationalist theologian at the University of Copenhagen and a liberal politician.

23. St. Ansgar (ca. 801-65), archbishop of Hamburg and Bremen, is credited with having introduced Christianity into Denmark.

24. N. F. S. Grundtvig, "Til Ansgars Minde" [In Memory of Ansgar] (1865), originally published in *Sang-Værk* (1870) and subsequently in *Værker i Udvalg* [Selected Works], ed. Georg Christensen and Hal Koch, vol. III (Copenhagen: Gyldendal, 1942), pp. 452-54.

25. Andreas Gottlob Rudelbach (1792-1862) was an older friend of Peter Christian Kierkegaard, a respected theologian, and an early supporter of Grundtvig.

26. Letter from Juliane and Christiane Rudelbach to A. G. Rudelbach, dated April 5, 1831; cited from Carl Weltzer, *Peter og Søren Kierkegaard* [Peter and Søren Kierkegaard] (Copenhagen: Gad, 1936), p. 39.

27. Letter from Juliane and Christiane Rudelbach to A. G. Rudelbach, dated July 2, 1832; cited from Weltzer, *Peter og Søren Kierkegaard,* p. 45.

28. Letter from Juliane and Christiane Rudelbach to A. G. Rudelbach, dated August 18, 1832; cited from Baagø, *Magister Jacob Christian Lindberg,* p. 197, n. 41.

29. Letter from Juliane Rudelbach to A. G. Rudelbach, dated November 29, 1831; cited from Weltzer, *Peter og Søren Kierkegaard,* p. 41.

30. *Pap.* X² A 134 [*SKJP* 6516].

31. Letter from Juliane and Christiane Rudelbach to A. G. Rudelbach; cited without date (which was on or shortly after December 26, 1831) from Carl Weltzer, *Grundtvig og Søren Kierkegaard* [Grundtvig and Søren Kierkegaard] (Copenhagen: Gyldendal, 1952), p. 40.

32. *Københavnsposten,* November 11, 1831, cited in Baagø, *Magister Jacob Christian Lindberg,* p. 191.

33. Cited in paraphrase, Baagø, *Magister Jacob Christian Lindberg,* pp. 194-95.

34. Letter from Juliane and Christiane Rudelbach to A. G. Rudelbach, dated January 28, 1832; cited from Baagø, *Magister Jacob Christian Lindberg,* p. 173, n. 23.

35. Cf. Baagø, *Magister Jacob Christian Lindberg,* p. 194.

36. Baagø, *Magister Jacob Christian Lindberg,* p. 195.

37. Baagø, *Magister Jacob Christian Lindberg,* p. 194.

38. J. P. Mynster's letter to W. F. Engelbreth, dated May 5, 1832; cited from Baagø, *Magister Jacob Christian Lindberg,* p. 196.

39. Letter from the Rudelbach sisters to A. G. Rudelbach, dated May 5, 1832 (in the Danish Royal Library, Manuscript Department [Det kongelige Bibliotek, Håndskriftafdelingen], hereafter "KBHA," the New Royal Collection [Ny kongelige Samling] hereafter "NkS" 1543, 2⁰, Breve til Rudelbach).

40. *SV* VIII, pp. 96-97 [*KW* XIV, p. 104 *(Two Ages)*].

41. *Pap.* II A 469-70 [*SKJP* 2582-83].

42. *Pap.* V A 64 [*SKJP* 2593].

43. *Pap.* XI¹ A 219 [*SKJP* 3966].

44. *Pap.* X² A 619 [*SKJP* 6603].

45. Ane Sørensdatter Kierkegaard, née Lund (1768-1834), was the second wife of Michael Pedersen Kierkegaard and the mother of Søren Kierkegaard and six other children.

46. Kirstine Nielsdatter Kierkegaard, née Røyen (1758-1796), the sister of a business partner of M. P. Kierkegaard, was his first wife; the marriage was childless and was terminated after less than two years by her death.

47. [Anna] Henriette Lund (1829-1909) was Søren Kierkegaard's niece. The passage from her memoirs cited here is from *Erindringer fra Hjemmet* [Memories from Home] (Copenhagen: Gyldendal, 1909), pp. 19-20. All of Henriette Lund's memoirs relating to Søren Kierkegaard are available in English translation in Kirmmse, *Encounters with Kierkegaard,* pp. 150-75; for the passage cited here, see p. 152.

48. Lund, *Erindringer fra Hjemmet,* p. 20; see Kirmmse, *Encounters with Kierkegaard,* pp. 152-53.

49. Hans Brøchner, "Erindringer om Søren Kierkegaard" [Recollections about Søren Kierkegaard] (KBHA, *Additamenta* 415 d. 4⁰; see Kirmmse, *Encounters with Kierkegaard,* p. 228.

50. Frederik Hammerich, *Et Levnedsløb* [A Life], vol. I (Copenhagen: Forlagsbureauet i Kjøbenhavn, 1882), p. 59.

51. Eline Heramb Boisen (1813-71) was related to Søren Kierkegaard by marriage, as she was married to Peter Christian Kierkegaard's brother-in-law, Frederik Engelhardt Boisen.

52. P. Bojsen, *Budstikkens Udgiver, Præsten F. E. Bojsens Liv og Levned* [The Publisher of "The Messenger": The Story of Pastor F. E. Boisen's Life] (Horsens: Schønberg, 1883), p. 94.

53. Translator's note: Here Bukdahl makes a slip that cannot easily be corrected by the translator. His memory has played tricks on him, and he combines

two places in the northern part of the Danish island of Zealand: *Gilleleje,* a fishing village, and *Hillerød,* a sizable market town. It is true that Kierkegaard was staying in Gilleleje when his mother died in the summer of 1834, but his subsequent memory of his childhood vacation, cited here in the text, is of a stay in Hillerød.

54. *Pap.* II A 238 [*SKJP* 5331].

55. Cited in *Folkevennen,* December 7, 1855, p. 2, col. 2.

56. Hans Lassen Martensen, *Af mit Levnet* [From My Life], vol. I (Copenhagen: Gyldendal, 1882-83), pp. 78-79.

57. *SV* XII, p. 326 [*KW* XXI, p. 37 *(For Self-Examination)*].

58. *SV* XII pp. 333-34 [*KW* XXI, pp. 46-47 *(For Self-Examination)*].

59. The original is in KBHA, NkS 2656, 4^0, Bd. I, p. 98; it has also been published in Weltzer, *Peter og Søren Kierkegaard,* p. 121.

60. The Fengers were [Carl] Emil Fenger (1814-84), a politician and physician and [Johannes] Ferdinand Fenger (1805-61), a theologian, pastor, and disciple of Grundtvig. The Hammerichs were Frederik Hammerich (see Chapter Four, note 7) and his brother Martin [Johannes] Hammerich (1811-81), a philologist and educator who was influenced by National Liberalism, Grundtvig, and the Scandinavianist movement. Peter Rørdam (1806-83) was a pastor and a follower of Grundtvig. The source for the present account is Elise Lindberg, *Oplevelser nedskrevne af Elise Lindberg* [Experiences Written Down by Elise Lindberg], in Rigarkivet [Danish National Archives] (Privatarkiv n. 5817, kasse 3, C., Nr. 5), p. 43.

61. Vilhelm Birkedal, *Personlig Oplevelser i et langt Liv* [Personal Experiences from a Long Life], vol. II (Copenhagen: Karl Schønbergs Forlag, 1890), p. 85.

62. *Pap.* II A 223 [*SKJP* 1976].

63. *Pap.* III A 26 [*SKJP* 1026].

64. *Pap.* III A 54-55 [*SKJP* 5454-55].

65. *Pap.* III A 56 [*SKJP* 5456].

66. *Pap.* III A 73 [*SKJP* 5468]. In the passage cited in the text, Kierkegaard's "task" and his father's "last wish" apparently refer to Kierkegaard's obligation to complete his theological studies.

67. *Pap.* III A 87 [*SKJP* 229].

68. *Pap.* III A 83 [*SKJP* 5475].

69. *Pap.* III A 84 [*SKJP* 5476].

Notes to Chapter Five

1. In a letter from C. C. Boisen to A. G. Rudelbach, dated July 31, 1832, Mynster is cited as having said this to archdeacon Rasmus Møller. There is a lacuna in the manuscript at the point where Bukdahl adds "fights for." The original is in KBHA, NkS 3813, 4⁰ and is cited in Baagø, *Magister Jacob Christian Lindberg*, p. 196n.

2. Johan Nicolai Madvig (1804-86) was a professor of classics at the University of Copenhagen and one of Kierkegaard's teachers. He was one of the leading Latinists of the nineteenth century.

3. Johan Ludvig Heiberg (1791-1860) was Denmark's leading playwright, critic, and aesthetician from the 1820s until the early 1840s. From the late 1820s until his death, Heiberg held important positions at the Royal Theatre. Johanne Luise Heiberg (1812-90) was for many years the leading lady of the Danish stage; she married Johan Ludvig Heiberg in 1831.

4. Hans and Trine and Jochum and Lisbeth are the principal couples in Johan Ludvig Heiberg's plays *Aprilsnarrene* [The April Fools] (1826) and *En Søndag paa Amager* [A Sunday on Amager] (1848), respectively.

5. *SV* X, p. 336 [*KW* XVII, p. 317 *(The Crisis and a Crisis in the Life of an Actress)*]; the passage which Kierkegaard cites (in Latin) is from Tertullian, *Apologeticum* 50.

6. *SV* X, p. 335 [*KW* XVII, p. 316 *(The Crisis and a Crisis in the Life of an Actress)*].

7. *SV* X, p. 329 [*KW* XVII, p. 309 *(The Crisis and a Crisis in the Life of an Actress)*].

8. *SV* X, p. 342 [*KW* XVII, p. 323 *(The Crisis and a Crisis in the Life of an Actress)*].

9. Rasmus Nielsen (1809-84) was a professor of philosophy at the University of Copenhagen. For a time Kierkegaard entertained the notion that Nielsen might become his disciple and popularizer, but he subsequently abandoned the idea, while Nielsen did not.

10. Mrs. Gyllembourg, whose full name was Thomasine Buntzen Heiberg Gyllembourg-Ehrensvärd (1773-1856), was J. L. Heiberg's mother and an important prose author in her own right.

11. *SV* VIII, pp. 58-59 [*KW* XIV, pp. 61-62 *(Two Ages)*].

12. *SV* VIII, p. 63 [*KW* XIV, p. 66 *(Two Ages)*].

13. *SV* VIII, pp. 64-65 [*KW* XIV, pp. 68-69 *(Two Ages)*].

14. *SV* VIII, p. 73 [*KW* XIV, pp. 77-78 *(Two Ages)*].

15. *SV* VIII, p. 83 [*KW* XIV, p. 89 *(Two Ages)*].

16. *SV* VIII, pp. 83-84 [*KW* XIV, p. 89 *(Two Ages)*].

17. *SV* VIII, p. 76 [*KW* XIV, p. 81 *(Two Ages)*].

18. *SV* VIII, pp. 76-77 [*KW* XIV, pp. 81-82 *(Two Ages)*].

19. Author's note: See my article "Kierkegaard-narkomani" [Kierkegaard Narcomania], *Dansk Udsyn* (1959): 360-76.

20. *SV* VIII, pp. 86-87 [*KW* XIV, pp. 92-93 *(Two Ages)*].

21. *SV* VIII, p. 90 [*KW* XIV, p. 97 *(Two Ages)*].

22. *SV* VIII, p. 91 [*KW* XIV, p. 97 *(Two Ages)*].

23. *SV* VIII, pp. 96-97 [*KW* XIV, p. 104 *(Two Ages)*].

24. *SV* VIII, p. 99 [*KW* XIV, p. 107 *(Two Ages)*].

25. *SV* VIII, pp. 101-2 [*KW* XIV, p. 109 *(Two Ages)*].

26. *Pap.* IX A 206.

27. Johanne Luise Heiberg, *Et liv genoplevet i erindringen* [A Life Relived in Recollection], 5th ed., ed. Niels Birger Wamberg, vol. 1 (1841-42) (Copenhagen: Gyldendal, 1973), pp. 342-43.

28. Martensen, *Af mit Levnet,* vol. II, p. 31.

29. Frederik [Ludvig] Høedt (1820-85) and Michael Wiehe (1820-64) were leading actors at the Royal Danish Theatre.

Notes to Chapter Six

1. *SV* VII, pp. 105-6 [*KW* XII.1, pp. 130-31 *(Concluding Unscientific Postscript)*].

2. *SV* VII, pp. 129-32 [*KW* XII.1, pp. 156-60 *(Concluding Unscientific Postscript)*].

3. *SV* VII, p. 342 [*KW* XII.1, p. 394 *(Concluding Unscientific Postscript)*].

4. *SV* VII, p. 149 [*KW* XII.1, p. 179 *(Concluding Unscientific Postscript)*].

5. *SV* VII, p. 537 [*KW* XII.1, p. 617 *(Concluding Unscientific Postscript)*]. In the passages cited in the text, "he" refers to Johannes Climacus, the pseudonym to whom Kierkegaard attributed *Concluding Unscientific Postscript.*

6. *SV* VII, p. 150 [*KW* XII.1, pp. 180-81 *(Concluding Unscientific Postscript)*].

7. *SV* VII, pp. 191-92 [*KW* XII.1, pp. 227-28 *(Concluding Unscientific Postscript)*].

8. *SV* VII, p. 252 [*KW* XII.1, p. 294 *(Concluding Unscientific Postscript)*].

9. *SV* VII, p. 332 [*KW* XII.1, p. 383 *(Concluding Unscientific Postscript)*].

10. *SV* VII, p. 432 [*KW* XII.1, p. 498 *(Concluding Unscientific Postscript)*].

11. *SV* VII, p. 486 [*KW* XII.1, p. 557 *(Concluding Unscientific Postscript)*].

12. *SV* VII, pp. 528-29 [*KW* XII.1, pp. 606-7 *(Concluding Unscientific Postscript)*].

Notes to Chapter Seven

1. Martensen, *Den christelige Dogmatik,* p. iii.

2. Peder Ludvig Møller (1814-65) was a Danish writer, poet, and literary critic. He was for a time closely associated with Goldschmidt and *The Corsair,* particularly during that journal's attack on Kierkegaard.

3. Meïr Aron Goldschmidt (1819-87) was an author, journalist, and editor of *Corsaren* [The Corsair] from October 1840 to October 1846, with whom Kierkegaard had a well-known conflict in 1845-46.

4. J. L. A. Kolderup-Rosenvinge (1798-1850) was a legal historian at the University of Copenhagen and a friend and walking companion of Kierkegaard.

5. Cited in Weltzer, *Grundtvig og Søren Kierkegaard,* p. 56.

6. Henrik Hertz (1797-1870) was a Danish poet, playwright, and aesthetician of the Heiberg school.

7. [Peter Martin] Orla Lehmann (1810-70) was a student politician when he and Kierkegaard were enrolled in the University of Copenhagen and subsequently a leader of the National Liberal Party.

8. Cf. *Pap.* X⁵ B 40, p. 258 [*KW* XX, p. 301 *(Practice in Christianity)*].

9. [Sophie] Henriette ["Jette"] Glahn Kierkegaard (1809-81) was Peter Christian Kierkegaard's second wife; she was bedridden for much of her adult life.

10. *SV* VI, pp. 453-54 [*KW* XI, p. 488 *(Stages on Life's Way)*].

11. Israel Levin (1810-83) was a linguist, lexicographer, man of letters, and Kierkegaard's personal secretary for a number of years. His recollections of Kierkegaard are in KBHA, Søren Kierkegaard Archiv, D. Pk. 5, "Hr. Cand. I. Levins Udtalelser om S. Kierkegaard 1858 og 1869" [Remarks by Mr. I. Levin, B. A., Concerning S. Kierkegaard, 1858 and 1869]). For an English language translation of Levin's recollections, see Kirmmse, *Encounters with Kierkegaard,* pp. 205-13, especially pp. 207-8.

12. Grímur Thomsen (1820-96) was an Icelandic poet and literary historian.

13. The dedicatory lines are published in H. P. Rohde, ed., *Auktionsprotokol over Søren Kierkegaards Bogsamling* [Auctioneer's List of the Library of Søren Kierkegaard] (Copenhagen: The Royal Library, 1967), pp. 87-88.

14. Steen Steensen Blicher (1772-1848) was a Danish writer best known for his short stories and poems.

15. *SV* XIII, p. 61 [*KW* I, p. 69 *(From the Papers of One Still Living)*].

16. *SV* IV, p. 407 [*KW* VIII, pp. 140-41 *(The Concept of Anxiety)*].

17. *Pap.* IX A 288, pp. 161-62 [*SKJP* 6254].

18. *Pap.* IX A 298 [*SKJP* 6259].

19. *Pap.* IX A 340 [*SKJP* 1016].

20. Kierkegaard came to associate the preaching of true Christianity with what he termed the "double danger," that is, the danger of being persecuted by the authorities and, in addition to this, the danger of being misunderstood by everyone.

21. *Pap.* IX A 381 [*SKJP* 6270].

22. *Pap.* X^1 A 132 [*SKJP* 693].

23. Cited from Martin Luther's *En christelig Postille* [A Christian Book of Homilies], trans. and ed. Jørgen Thisted (Copenhagen, 1828).

24. *Pap.* X^1 A 133 [*SKJP* 4018].

25. *Pap.* X^1 A 135 [*SKJP* 236].

26. *Pap.* X^1 A 247 [*SKJP* 6382].

27. *Pap.* VIII^1 A 99 [*SKJP* 5998].

28. *Pap.* VIII^1 A 544 [*SKJP* 6105].

29. *Pap.* VIII^1 A 233 [*SKJP* 6039].

30. *Pap.* VIII^1 A 553.

31. *Pap.* VIII^1 A 452 [*SKJP* 6085].

32. *Pap.* X^1 A 322 [*SKJP* 6396].

33. *Pap.* X^1 A 407 [*SKJP* 4861].

34. *Pap.* X^1 A 632 [*SKJP* 4163].

35. *Pap.* X^1 A 676 [*SKJP* 6486].

36. *Pap.* X^2 A 88 [*SKJP* 6504].

37. *Pap.* X^2 A 48 [*SKJP* 6498].

38. *Pap.* X^3 A 13 [*SKJP* 6611].

39. *Pap.* X^3 A 714 [*SKJP* 991].

40. *Pap.* X^2 A 341 [*SKJP* 2793].

41. *Pap.* XI^1 A 234, p. 189 [*SKJP* 2971].

42. *Pap.* XI^1 A 473 [*SKJP* 3589].

43. *Pap.* XI^2 A 149 [*SKJP* 2082].

44. *Pap.* XI^1 A 532 [*SKJP* 3182].

45. Frederik Dreier (1827-53) was an early Danish radical and declared socialist.

46. Cf. Chapter Three, note 10.

47. *Pap.* X^2 A 251 [*SKJP* 6548].

48. *Pap.* X^2 A 399, p. 284.

49. *Pap.* X^2 A 401 [*SKJP* 4555].

50. *SV* XIII, p. 546 [*KW* XXII, p. 60 *(The Point of View for My Work as an Author)*].

51. *SV* XIII, p. 574 [*KW* XXII, p. 90 *(The Point of View for My Work as an Author)*].

Notes to Chapter Eight

1. Brandes, *Søren Kierkegaard*, p. 359.

2. Brandes, *Søren Kierkegaard*, p. 361.

3. *SV* XIV, p. 72 [*KW* XXIII, p. 62 *(The Moment and Late Writings)*].

4. *SV* XIV, p. 79 [*KW* XXIII, p. 68 *(The Moment and Late Writings)*].

5. Author's note: It is true that the article about the second printing of *Practice* retracts the possibility of an "admission," but this is only with respect to any attempt at using an admission to rescue the established church. As a requirement for individual honesty, the insistence on an admission remains in effect.

6. *SV* XIV, p. 81 [*KW* XXIII, p. 70 *(The Moment and Late Writings)*].

7. The article in question appeared in *Fædrelandet* on May 26, 1855, and is reprinted in *SV* XIV, pp. 93-100 [*KW* XXIII, pp. 79-85 *(The Moment and Late Writings)*].

8. *SV* XIV, pp. 98-99 [*KW* XXIII, pp. 83-84 *(The Moment and Late Writings)*].

9. Author's note: "This Must Be Said, So Let It Be Said, Then" appeared simultaneously with the first issue of *The Moment*. This pamphlet explains the intention of the "awakening" presented in *The Moment* as well as the category within which this awakening was to be understood. The intention was: Refrain from the official worship of God. The category is: Act on your own responsibility, I cannot obligate you to anything definite (cf. *SV* XIV, pp. 85ff. [*KW* XXIII, pp. 73-78 *(The Moment and Late Writings)*]. The first issue of *The Moment* (and, in a way, the subsequent issues as well) can be regarded as one long commentary on "This Must Be Said," since the same thing is hammered in again and again (cf. *SV* XIV, pp. 107, 180, 250ff., 324f., 328 [*KW* XXIII, pp. 93, 168, 235-36, 312, 316 *(The Moment and Late Writings)*]).

10. *SV* XIV, p. 120 [*KW* XXIII, p. 108 *(The Moment and Late Writings)*].

11. *Pap.* XI^3 B 179-96 [*KW* XXIII, pp. 563-80 *(The Moment and Late Writings)*].

12. Just Henrik Paulli (1809-65) was the chaplain at the Royal Palace Church, Bishop Mynster's son-in-law, and a good friend of H. L. Martensen.

13. Ludvig J. M. Gude (1820-95) was a cleric and a good friend of H. L. Martensen.

14. Hans L. Martensen, *Biskop H. Martensens Breve* [The Letters of Bishop

H. Martensen], ed. Bjørn Kornerup, vol. I, *Breve til L. Gude, 1848-1859* [Letters to L. Gude, 1848-1859] (Copenhagen: Gad, 1955), pp. 142-43.

15. *SV* XIV, p. 221 [*KW* XXIII, p. 207 *(The Moment and Late Writings)*].

16. *SV* XIV, pp. 221-22 [*KW* XXIII, p. 207 *(The Moment and Late Writings)*].

17. *SV* XIV, p. 300 [*KW* XXIII, p. 290 *(The Moment and Late Writings)*].

18. *SV* XII, p. 131 [*KW* XX, p. 141 *(Practice in Christianity)*].

19. *SV* XIV, p. 52 [*KW* XXIII, p. 46 *(The Moment and Late Writings)*].

20. Brandes, *Søren Kierkegaard*, p. 357.

21. *SV* XIV, p. 54 [*KW* XXIII, p. 48 *(The Moment and Late Writings)*].

22. *SV* XIV, p. 55 [*KW* XXIII, p. 49 *(The Moment and Late Writings)*].

23. See Brøchner's remarks on Kierkegaard during the attack on the church in Kirmmse, *Encounters with Kierkegaard*, pp. 247-48.

24. *SV* XIII, p. 497 [*KW* XXII, p. 9 *(On My Work as an Author)*].

25. *Pap.* XI^3 B 155, p. 249 [*KW* XXIII, p. 587 *(The Moment and Late Writings)*].

26. *Pap.* XI^3 B 142, p. 227 [*KW* XXIII, pp. 533-34 *(The Moment and Late Writings)*].

27. *Pap.* XI^3 B 91, pp. 145-46.

28. *Pap.* XI^3 B 19, p. 49.

29. Cf. *SV* IX, pp. 327-39 [*KW* XVI, pp. 345-58 *(Works of Love)*].

30. *Pap.* XI^3 B 82, pp. 128-29 [*KW* XXIII, pp. 494-95 *(The Moment and Late Writings)*].

31. *Pap.* XI^3 B 43 [*SKJP* 3068].

32. *Pap.* XI^3 B 44:4.

33. Cf. *Pap.* XI^3 B 43, p. 86 [*SKJP* 3068].

34. *SV* VII, p. 532 [*KW* XII.1, pp. 610-11 *(Concluding Unscientific Postscript)*].

35. *Pap.* X^2 A 299 [*SKJP* 4550].

36. *SV* XIV, p. 352 [*KW* XXIII, p. 341 *(The Moment and Late Writings)*].

37. *SV* XIV, p. 353 [*KW* XXIII, p. 342 *(The Moment and Late Writings)*].

38. *SV* XIV, pp. 355-56 [*KW* XXIII, p. 345 *(The Moment and Late Writings)*].

39. *SV* XIV, pp. 356-57 [*KW* XXIII, pp. 346-47 *(The Moment and Late Writings)*].

40. *Pap.* XI^2 A 439, p. 440 [*SKJP* 6969].

41. Cf. Hanne Mourier's and Raphael Meyer's accounts of their interviews with Regine Schlegel, née Olsen, in her old age in Kirmmse, *Encounters with Kierkegaard*, pp. 38, 42.

42. Eggert Christopher Tryde (1781-1850) was archdeacon of the Church of Our Lady.

43. See Henriette Lund's memoirs in Kirmmse, *Encounters with Kierkegaard,* p. 173.

44. Rasmus Nielsen. See Chapter Five, note 9.

45. Peter Michael Stilling (1812-69) was a writer on philosophical and theological subjects, influenced by Kierkegaard.

46. Martensen, *Biskop H. Martensens Breve,* vol. I, pp. 151-52.

47. Hans Adolph Brorson (1694-1764) was a Danish poet and hymn writer.

48. *B&A* I, p. 20 [*KW XXV,* p. 27 *(Letters and Documents)*].

Index

153